SEASONS OF CHANGE

SEASONS OF CHANGE

TURNING POINTS IN A JOURNEY OF FAITH

PERRY G.H. SOH

© Copyright 2020 – Perry G.H. Soh
All rights reserved.

This book may not be copied or reprinted for commercial gain or profit.

Unless otherwise indicated Scripture quotations are from the New International Version of the Bible.
THE HOLY BIBLE, NEW INTERNATIONAL VERSION®, NIV®
Copyright © 1995 by Zondervan Corporation. Used by permission.
All rights reserved worldwide.

Cover Design: Kory Kwok
Book Layout: Angie Wagler

ISBN: 9798675325818

DEDICATION

First and foremost, I dedicate this book to the God and Father of our Lord Jesus Christ. If not for His prompting to "Go and write a book" on the day I was to be discharged from the hospital after my heart surgery, this book would not have been written.

I also dedicate "Seasons of Change" to my dear wife, Catherine, who has stood by me through thick and thin in all the seasons we have been together. Thank you for your fervent love, consistent prayer and unwavering support.

Lastly, I dedicate this book to our two sons and daughters-in-law, Joo-Lip & Lynnette and Joo-Meng & Rosanna. You have blessed us with 12 grandchildren and we are trusting the Lord to guard, lead and guide your families with the hope that each generation may surpass the previous generation in the work of God's kingdom on earth. Do not forget our family motto: *"As for me and my house, we will serve the Lord."*

ACKNOWLEDGEMENTS

People need people. Whether we realize it or not, we are influenced and directed by the people who come into our lives at different junctures of our journey. Some may have inspired us to rise beyond ourselves while others may have helped us—either through a word of encouragement or in practical ways—to succeed in what we endeavour to do to have a better life.

I am grateful to the people in my life who have contributed in one way or another to my well-being. As mentioned in my memoir, there were many who played a part in prompting me to step up and grow with change. I thank all of you for your friendship and caring heart; especially those who walked along with me in good times and in times of need.

The church has been a large part of life for Catherine and me. We are thankful for the church family at Life-Spring, for the privilege of serving with you and the other leaders in the work of advancing God's Kingdom locally and through missions abroad. You have enriched our lives with your love, prayer and support.

Finally, I must acknowledge two sisters-in-Christ, Grace

Chik and Liz Chua, who did most of the editing. Thank you for motivating me to press on till the book was completed. The first book you authored and published in your spare time was a great inspiration for me!

Note: "Season's Blessings For You: A Collection of Christmas Stories" by Grace Chik was published in 2010. "A Century: A Family Story" by Liz Chua was published in 2011.

TABLE OF CONTENTS

Foreword		11
Prologue		17
Introduction		21
Chapter 1	A Turning Point in Hospital	25
Chapter 2	Let Your Light Shine	37
Chapter 3	Hope in Place of Hopelessness	43
Chapter 4	A New Phase of Change	51
Chapter 5	Venture into Business	59
Chapter 6	Changing Pace	69
Chapter 7	Birthing A New Church	75
Chapter 8	Spiritual Revival	87
Chapter 9	A Second Chance	97
Chapter 10	Revival Tensions	101
Chapter 11	Church Split	109
Chapter 12	Encounter with Jesus	119
Chapter 13	Breakthrough with A New Name	129
Chapter 14	Empowered for Outreach	135
Chapter 15	Be Fruitful and Multiply	159

FOREWORD

Seasons of Change is a reader-friendly book. Written in a free-flowing style, you can read this book through one sitting. Author Perry Soh invites you to travel with him on his life journey.

The first milestone occurred when at the age of 21, Perry's father unexpectedly died. He then had to support himself and his family. This led him to search for God. He encountered Jesus at a local Methodist Church. That was a massive turning point as he discovered he had God as his Father and Guide.

His first job was with Straits Times, the national newspaper of Singapore. For four years, he courted Catherine his work-mate. Fully conscious of his humble family roots, he even suggested that she should marry another man with better family connections! However, with his future mother-in-law's prompting, engagement and marriage followed.

In 1976, Perry and Catherine uprooted themselves from Singapore and immigrated to Toronto, Canada. His first employment was with a lampshade-making factory. He was petrified whilst handling the sharp saws which cut through thick plastic sheets. On the fourth day, when he saw one of his boss' hands as a mere stump, he resigned in fear.

Perry's journey in the world of business led him to 12 different jobs. Like Joseph in ancient Egypt, he found great favor with his employers. One even offered him a higher salary than what Perry had asked for. Another enrolled him for a course on public speaking. This enabled him to flourish as a salesman and communicator. Perry had an insatiable appetite to learn and grow. He gained remarkable skills in printing, graphic arts, sales, advertising and management. Finally, a client urged him to launch his own graphics and advertising agency. This led to the establishment of Dynacom, a company he owned and managed for over a decade.

The second half of his book is devoted to Perry's involvement with the local church. First, he served as a deacon, and later as an elder in Bridlegrove Church. In the early 1980s, a new church fellowship was birthed in Toronto comprising mainly of Christians from Singapore and Malaysia. Perry and his family decided to invest their time and energy to the fledgling Malaysian-Singaporean Bible Church (MSBC). This congregation grew by leaps and bounds.

1992 brought MSBC and Perry to a crossroad. Joe Ozawa, a clinical psychologist was invited to speak in the church. His laidback style and his "soft" voice endeared him to his listeners. When he made his appeal, many young people stepped to the front for prayer. To everyone's amazement, folks began to shake; some overwhelmed by the Spirit, fell to the ground. Many were weeping tears of repentance and joy. This shook the entire church!

Questions were raised. Was this of God or was it from a dark source? The leaders decided to put a lid over these strange manifestations. They adopted a wait-and-see strategy but found it difficult to hold the newly-found enthusiasm of the younger members with the conservatism of the older ones. For nearly nine years, they decided to continue with their traditional style of worship and church life.

The younger generation were in the meantime hungry for the Spirit's infilling and empowering. In 1994, Toronto Airport Christian Fellowship was in a revival and the fire of God was blazing fiercely. MSBC young leaders were impacted. They had their own gatherings with lively worship. And they were exercising spiritual gifts like prophecy and tongues. You can hear two strident roars—"Go for it!" and "Stop it!"

In a candid chapter, Perry pin-pointed to four major lacks in MSBC—the lack of unity (tensions between older and younger members); lack of growth (the cells operated as comfortable cliques); lack of transparency (deep hurts and pains were suppressed); and lack of outreach (the direction of the church was more "come" than "go").

Things inevitably came to a head in 2003. The church split. Those who remained in MSBC were the younger members supported by the new lead pastor Alvin Koh and older leaders like Perry. They brought into the "new" church, speakers from Singing Waters and other leading ministries. They ministered lovingly to the leaders who in turn participated in training courses enabling them to move freely in the Spirit. A number experienced deliverance from oppressive spirits followed by inner healing. The leaders also invited trainers from Evangelism Explosion to equip their members to share the gospel effectively.

In 2004, the leaders proposed a name-change. In keeping with cosmopolitan Toronto and in the wake of new-found vitality, the name "Life Spring" was adopted. With the new name, Life-Spring began to partner with other churches in praying for the city, feeding the homeless and street people. Church planting and missions featured high on their agenda. When Perry retired from his business, he served as pastor to the young church plant in Mississauga. Today several of the "younger generation" at Life-Spring are exercising key leadership roles including Gabriel Wee, the current Lead Pastor.

Perry ends his book with the theme of *fruitfulness*. He equates this with re-production. In the realm of the natural, his two sons and their wives produced 12 children. In the supernatural sphere, Perry and Catherine rejoiced that all their family members are walking with the Lord. Their joy increased when they and other Life-Spring members are actively encouraging and equipping younger believers to grow in spiritual maturity and fruitfulness.

Seasons of Change has many lessons to teach the wider church. We can see some of the distinctive times of **Ecclesiastes 3:1-8** reflected in Perry's life story. There are distinctive times for planting and uprooting, tearing down and building up. Change, as Perry shared with us, is always uncomfortable but rightly adopted and acted upon leads to new adventures and untold blessings.

CHUA WEE HIAN
LONDON, UK, JULY 2020

Rev. Chua Wee Hian was the General Secretary of the International Fellowship of Evangelical Students (1972-1991). He was the Founding and Senior Pastor of Emmanuel Evangelical Church in Westminster, London (1991-2008), and author of "Learning to Lead, Dear Mum and Dad" and "Getting Through Customs" (published by IVP) and "Ever Blessing, Ever Blessed" (Zacc. Press).

PROLOGUE

Life is like going on a journey. We begin this journey the moment we're born and end it the moment we die. Between these two moments are certain milestones we're expected to cross, marking our progress along the way. Such points of our lives may include getting a higher education, landing a job, marrying the one you love, raising children, buying a house, becoming grandparents, and retiring from the workforce. We do the best we can, being aware that we will face detours or roadblocks that may distract or deter us from where we wish to be as we move from one milestone to the next. Even though we're uncertain where our journey will finally end, we press on because that's what everyone is expected to do.

Occasionally, we may slow down to rest but not for long because we don't want to fall behind as we see other hard-pressed travellers also on the move either beside or ahead of us. As we continue our journey, we realize that there are many crossroads that make us wonder at times if we've lost our way. We know we need help to make the right turns or change our course to stay on track but we're afraid to ask. No matter how rough the terrain or how difficult the road conditions, stopping is not always an option for life might stop when we come to a standstill.

I'm a fellow traveller like you and millions of people around the world. Before road maps were charted to help travellers find their way, compasses were used by earlier travellers to point the general direction they must go. Today, we have the GPS (Global Positioning System) that can pinpoint the position we're in and where we need to turn or change course to keep us from going astray. However, in real life, there is no road map or compass or GPS that can give us the assurance that we're always heading in the right direction, never afraid that we will lose control and crash along the way. It's for this reason that I'm motivated to write this book; to share what I've experienced in my journey in the hope that I could help my fellow travellers to look out for turning points that can come at different stages of their lives that could change the course of their journey for good.

Even though this is only a memoir of one man's journey, I hope what I share can be applied to others going through some similar paths in their journey. It may be a thought or a word, an incident or an idea that triggers a change in the mind. If that leads to a better choice of living then I'm thankful for the opportunity to act as a signpost for those who may have momentarily lost their way.

I believe all travellers, young or old, need some kind of signposts to assure them that they're heading in the right direction and to guide them toward the destination they hope to go. As you will read from the narratives, I was

PROLOGUE

fortunate to have seen many of the signposts at various stages of my life to know where my final destination will be. I hope that you too will find the route to your final destination. After all, isn't this the most important part of our life journey?

INTRODUCTION

During a week-end visit to our older son's home, Joo-Lip asked if I would like to have a bike ride with five of his children along a country trail in Erin. He would drop us at the start of the trail and pick us up at the other end.

I immediately said "Yes" although I had some concern about five-year old Olivia: could she catch up with the group? However, when I began riding from the starting point, I was gasping and finding it hard to catch up.

"Slow down," I yelled out to the older kids, trying to catch my breath. I must admit that it was with great difficulty and a sigh of relief that we finally reached our destination some five km. away. Believe it or not, Olivia was the first person to reach the end of the trail!

The following week, this time visiting our younger son in Mississauga, Joo-Meng asked me when we were going on our cruise.

"End of October," I replied.

In conversation, I shared about my biking experience admitting with a little embarrassment that I was unable to catch up even with a five-year old. My son advised me to have my heart checked by a cardiologist before the cruise and, as a doctor at the Trillium Health Centre, he would arrange an appointment as soon as he could.

I knew that I was recently experiencing shortness of breath when mowing the lawn at home. Apart from this, I had no health issues. I was an active person, eating sensibly and living a healthy and balanced life-style. Lack of stamina, I thought, might be why I was short of breath; got to take up jogging or join a gym soon to build my stamina again.

When I checked in at Trillium Health Centre on a Wednesday (September 23, 2013), on the instruction of my cardiologist, I was told that I needed an angiogram to see if there was any blockage which might explain the shortness of breath and sudden rise in my blood pressure. The bad news came when I awoke from sedation on a hospital bed. Dr. Randy Watson, my cardiologist, explained that the angiogram showed severe blockages in two main coronary arteries and two subsidiary arteries. I urgently needed a coronary artery bypass and he would set up the appointment for the following Monday.

Being hooked onto a monitoring system 24/7 with regular checks by the nursing staff made me realize how critical a condition I was in. Joo-Meng told me that surgery was the only option to survive. He assured me that I was in good hands. Trillium has a highly qualified and experienced team of heart surgeons performing this operation on a regular basis.

"What am I to do?" I was expected to conduct a wedding

INTRODUCTION

ceremony the following Saturday for a young couple whom my wife and I had been counselling for the past ten months in preparation for this big day. Moreover, my wife and I had booked a cruise leaving next month with a group from the church. I was prepared to forego the cruise, paying the penalty for cancellation, but what about the wedding?

"Could I have the surgery after the wedding?" I asked Dr. Watson

"No."

"Could I leave the hospital for a couple of days to attend to some business before the surgery?"

"No" was his firm answer.

I felt like a prisoner being confined to a hospital bed day and night. At the same time, I was thankful as I reflected on what had been happening in the past two weeks and what could have happened if my problem hadn't been discovered in time.

TIMELY INTERVENTION

Were it not for the bike ride and the timely appointment made with Dr. Watson, I would have faced the imminent danger of having a heart attack due to the rich and plentiful food served on the cruise ship. It's from this point of view that I saw the intervening hand of God. It's from this perspective that I'm thankful for His grace in sparing me the threat of what has been called a 'silent killer', which apparently strikes thousands of unknowing

North Americans each year because of bad cholesterol and high blood pressure that cause blockages in their coronary system.

I'm prompted to write this book to share my story. A story that is inspired by my 10 days of confinement, deeply touched by the excellent health care I received from all the staff at Trillium. A story that must necessarily include a testimony of God's intervening hand at various stages of my life since I was saved from the pit of hopelessness at the age of 21 after my father's sudden death. A story that needs to embrace the church given my involvement for the last 39 years—serving first as a deacon, then as an elder, and later as a pastor—overseeing its growth from the start-up stage to where it is today. A story that hopefully will be an inspiration for the next generation, motivating the young people to seek and serve God because He truly is the Source and Sustainer of life.

Ten days. It took only ten days to turn my world upside down or should I say right-side up. I know I'm going through a season of change. A new season that will give me a greater sensitivity of my role as husband, father, grandfather, church leader and pastor. A greater measure of gratitude and appreciation for my family as well as the spiritual family in my church, and for people who the Lord puts in my path. A greater zeal for living.

CHAPTER 1

A TURNING POINT IN HOSPITAL

Have you ever faced a health crisis that opened your eyes to the fact that you're a mortal being, more fragile and vulnerable than you think? Our health is something we often take for granted, as well as many other things that affect our well-being, until they're taken away from us. Whether we're prepared or not, sickness can suddenly hit and rob us of the things we enjoy in life. In our weakened state, the danger is to let the sickness rule our minds to the extent that our whole being (body, soul and spirit) is negatively affected. At such a time, it is wise to recognize that we need help both physically and spiritually to stay on course in our journey.

Cardiac surgery can be a traumatic and risky operation, cutting open the sternum in order to have access to the heart. In my case, the four-hour surgery involved fixing four coronary bypasses over a beating heart.

Even on my first day at Trillium, I recognized the privilege of being a patient in an Ontario hospital. I had a spacious private room with a window view of the street. The nurses were courteous and dedicated to their work even though most were working on 12-hour rotating shifts. In my view, the patient care was excellent. Even the hot-cooked meals were surprisingly good.

When I met Dr. C. Cutrara on my second day, he turned out to be the chief surgeon who was to perform my coronary artery bypass. He came across as a caring, competent and confident doctor when he assured me that the risk would be minimal (1 out of 100). My recovery would be fast because of my overall state of health. However, he strongly advised me to cancel the cruise.

There are some things most of us take for granted as Canadians, but given my ten-day stay as a cardiac patient at Trillium, I must say that it's a great blessing to live in Canada which has the best health care benefit in the world! No need to worry about the hospital expenses for such an intensive surgery because all expenses are covered by OHIP (Ontario Health Insurance Plan).

But that's only looking at the physical side. What about the anxious thoughts lurking at the back of my mind facing such a major operation?

I knew I was covered by prayer, lots of prayers, once the word got out that I had landed in the hospital. I was deeply touched when I spoke over the phone with Rachael, the bride-to-be; she told me that she and Adrian could hardly sleep the night they heard the news. While many were praying as soon as they were notified by word of mouth or email, Joseph Wee felt moved to call a day of fasting among his group prior to the day of the surgery. When she was notified about my surgery, Emerald, a friend and intercessor in Singapore, emailed to say she would go on a three-day fast to pray and intercede on my behalf. Those who could make it to the hospital came to visit and prayed over me.

Thanks to everyone who interceded for me, my eyes were suddenly opened to the power of prayer for I was kept in a place of peace and quiet most of the time. Moreover, God was working to strengthen my spirit sending different people to encourage me, based on my interactions or what I regard as "spiritual encounters" with the following nursing staff: [1]

Encounter #1: On the second night, after the shift change, Ms. A came into my room to inform me that she was to be my night nurse. When I was awakened at around 10 p.m. to have my regular checks (body temperature, blood pressure, heart rate), I asked her where she was from originally.

"Punjab, in northern India," she replied.

"Are most people from Punjab, Sikhs?" I asked.

"Yes, but I am a Christian," was her response.

Curious, I asked her, "How did you become a Christian?"

She said she grew up in a Christian home and her father is a pastor of a local church in Toronto. However, it was in

---

1. Note: Alphabets are used in the following narratives, substituting the names of the nurses to protect their identities.

India where she attended an evangelistic rally where Dr. Dinakaran spoke that she was truly saved as a result of a word—the only word she could remember—that pierced her heart, causing her to break into tears and weep for days thereafter as she started to speak in an unknown tongue.

"What was the word?" I asked.

"God loves you!"

Sensing her fervent spirit, I asked her to pray for me, mentioning that I am also a pastor serving the Lord in a local church. It was a divine moment as she held my hand and spontaneously prayed over me. What an uplifting experience to be blessed by the words of a nurse whom I hardly knew until she came on shift that night!

Encounter #2: Ms. B was a day nurse who came on duty on the fourth day of my stay at Trillium, still hooked up and monitored 24/7 in the same private room. I noticed the moment she arrived that she was quite a friendly and outspoken lady but rather loud and overbearing in my view. I wanted to reach out to her.

"Do you have a word, Lord, which I could share with her that might help her to change?"

She had to work in another hospital the following day, so I didn't see her until she reported for duty on Monday, the day of my surgery scheduled for 1:30 p.m.

When she came into my room that morning, I was pleasantly surprised when she took a seat facing me near the window where I was sitting on a reclining chair.

I asked her, "How was your weekend?"

"Horrible!" she replied.

"What happened?"

She described her experience with two of her patients in the other hospital—one an alcoholic, and the other a drug addict—who gave her a hard time even though she was trying her best to attend to their needs. Inserting an IV-lead onto the hand of the alcoholic was a huge challenge because he promptly pulled it out, three times in a row.

"Why are people like that?" she asked me.

"The simple answer is that they do not know God," I replied.

She told me that she had been reading a book, titled 'Purpose-Driven Life', given to her by a colleague and had felt in her heart that there was something missing in her life. She was interested in continuing our conversation but had to attend to her nursing duties first since she had just started her morning shift.

I could sense B's desire to know more about God. She had a busy morning and I had to pray that she would not miss the opportunity to resume our conversation. Catherine, my dear wife and love companion, arrived an hour later and when B popped her head into my room, she cheerily said,

"We have a date, I'm coming soon!"

I had two Scriptures in mind to share with B, and was glad that Catherine had brought her Bible with her. The two Scriptures were:

John 1:12-13 *"Yet to all who received him, to those who believed in his name, he gave the right to become children of God—children born not of natural descent, nor of human decision or a husband's will, but born of God."*

John 14:15-18 *"And I will ask the Father, and he will give you another Counselor to be with you forever—the Spirit of truth. The world cannot accept him, because it neither sees him nor knows him. But you know him, for he lives with you and will be in you."*

When B dropped in again, she took a chair and sat between the two of us. After showing her the two Scriptures, I explained to B that in order to know God, she needed to have a relationship with Him through His Son, Jesus Christ; she also needed to have the Holy Spirit to be born again.

"Would you like to receive Jesus to enter into a relationship with God and would you like to receive the Holy Spirit this morning to be filled with His love, joy and peace?"

"Yes" was her eager response.

So we led her through a prayer not only to receive Jesus Christ as her Saviour but also the Holy Spirit as her Counselor. She expressed her joy when she left my room and later came to give us a hug before I was wheeled downstairs into the Operation Room.

What a joy and encouragement to see a soul saved and seemingly touched in her spirit in such a short time! Just before I went into surgery; a divine moment to show that God was with us even in the hospital!

Encounter #3: After my surgery, I was moved into another floor where I was to be kept under observation. Ms. C, a nurse, came into my room and excitedly shared with Catherine and me how she came to know our son, Dr. Soh.

"One day, I was praying when God impressed upon me that I should pray for a certain doctor at Trillium. He even showed me his picture in my mind. I resisted for a while, asking why I should pray for someone I didn't know. Later, I saw this doctor approaching along the corridor, and recognizing him as the one I saw during my prayer, I started to pray for him. That was how I got to know Dr. Soh."

Isn't God amazing to provide an intercessor for our son even at his workplace? Is this part of His plan to give him boldness to openly identify himself as a Christian doctor among his colleagues at Trillium? C told us that she is thinking of applying for registration as a hospital chaplain so she could pray openly for others as a Christian.

Encounter #4: A few days later I was transferred to another private room with a window view looking down to the car-park. Observing the visitors from this vantage point, all coming in with a concerned look on their face, no doubt anxious about the condition of their loved ones in the hospital, what I saw in my mind was a picture of sacrificial love in motion. Whether it was a husband or a wife, a son or a daughter, a relative or a friend, all were at the hospital sacrificially spending time to be at the bedside of their loved ones, no matter how busy they were or how inconvenient it was for them to come.

On the third day, I was awakened by the night nurse at around 10 p.m. to have my regular checks.

"Where did you come from originally?" I asked Ms. D as she checked my blood pressure.

"I was born in India and had worked as a nurse in Saudi Arabia for a number of years. I have two daughters, now 18 and 16. Even though the money was good, my husband and I left Saudi to migrate to Canada over ten years ago because I felt the culture there was too repressive, especially for my young daughters."

She told me she was a Christian and, based on her recommendation, thirty nurses from her home country were given similar employment in Saudi after she left. I commended her for her good work and was moved to give her a word of blessing, which she gladly accepted. What a joy to meet someone like her with such an inspiring story, lifting my spirit even while I was lying flat on a hospital bed!

A SECOND CHANCE

My ten-day stay at Trillium was a life-changing experience, like being given "a second chance" in the words of David Burns, a volunteer who came to participate in an educational talk for the benefit of the heart patients and their family members. This was what he shared (in his own words) with the patients in the class.

"Hi, my name is Dave Burns and I'm the Team Leader at Trillium for a group of volunteers called Healing Hearts Volunteers. We are all cardiac surgery graduates having

A TURNING POINT IN HOSPITAL

experienced either bypass or valve surgery. Our job is to make ourselves available to cardiac patients and their families where we share our stories and answer questions from the perspective of someone who has "been there".

In my case, at age fifty-five, I suffered a serious heart attack in 2001 and was transported by ambulance to Trillium Emergency. I was very lucky not to die. I endured multiple cardiac arrests in the first few hours that I was in the hospital. Thanks to the ER and CCU staff I did survive and had angioplasty done for my worst blockage. However my stent failed after three years and in 2004 I had a quintuple bypass surgery (five grafts) by Dr. Bhatnagar. It has been very successful in maintaining my quality of life for almost ten years. I am able to do almost anything you would expect a healthy person of my age to be able to do. Because of this "second chance" I have been able to participate in family moments that I might have missed. I was able to present my son with his engineering iron ring at graduation, saw him get married, walked my daughter down the aisle, and experienced the arrival in the last few years of three beautiful grandchildren. My father never got to meet his grandchildren. He died at age 52 from his second heart attack.

With heart disease you can't control your family history or your age. You can control and do something about weight, smoking, diet, exercise, blood pressure, stress, cholesterol and other lifestyle choices. The choice is yours.

Most of all, try to enjoy this extra time you've been given. I use part of my time to pay it back and pay it forward by volunteering at Trillium. I have been doing this for twelve years and it has been a wonderful, gratifying experience for me."

QUALITY HEALTH CARE TAKES DEDICATION AND TEAMWORK

My senses were quickened as I became increasingly aware of the care and attention I was receiving as a cardiac patient at Trillium. I could see that everyone was doing his or her best to serve the patients— the nurses and cleaners, the surgeon and cardiologist, the pharmacist and physiotherapist, the education information staff and volunteers—like a well-trained team working collaboratively to fulfill a corporate mission. A mission that appears to be driven by an open declaration of Trillium's goals and values as stated on the billboards for public viewing as follows:

"We are focused on delivering safe, quality and patient-centred care. We believe in health care that works for you. We believe in active participation of patients and families. We believe in quality and innovation. We believe in the power of teamwork. We promise to:

- Provide you with timely access to high quality care in a safe and comfortable environment

- Share meaningful information about your plan of care so you can make informed decisions

- Involve you and those most important to you in your care

- Listen and respond to your needs in order to build a trusting relationship

- Care for you with respect, compassion and dignity"

It was a wonderful privilege to have met so many good people at Trillium. Together, they have built a great reputation behind its vision to have "A new kind of health care for a healthier community."

Just as an organization needs a vision to work towards the goals it has set to optimize its performance, we too must set our sights on where we wish to go and what we hope to accomplish in our journey. However, we must also consider what is truly important lest we spend our lives chasing after lesser things that don't really matter at the end of our journey.

I know that my life would not be the same given what I went through—a health crisis as noted by a friend. The way I look at life now, it's more precious and redeeming, more dependent on God than self. It's like being given a second chance to change and have a better life. Things and relationships that I may have taken for granted, I can appreciate and enjoy so much more...such as my body that I need to take good care of in order to stay healthy and strong. I can certainly relate with the words of the prophet Jeremiah as he prayed to God acknowledging his utter dependence on him.

"I know, O Lord, that a man's life is not his own; it is not for man to direct his steps." (Jeremiah 10:23)

CHAPTER 2

LET YOUR LIGHT SHINE

There are times in our journey when we feel like we're in a rut and wish we could change our circumstances to live a more fruitful and purposeful life. We may seek to improve ourselves by upgrading our skills or education, hoping to gain recognition or have a higher status in our career or station of life. We strive to better ourselves, and it's frustrating at times to see so little change in spite of all our efforts. I think it's prudent to ask ourselves at such times, "What are we striving for; what good do we expect to see at the end of the road?" Change is good and should be encouraged if it leads to a better way of living.

I recognize that I have gone through many seasons of life-changes. Indeed, there were many turning points that have made me the person that I am today. Still a work in progress, I can see the hand of God shaping me even in my senior years.

I had sensed a forthcoming season of change when I spoke to the church family at Mississauga *Life-Spring* on September 1, 2013. I had no clue what was to come; it was simply an anticipation of better and greater things to follow. I certainly did not expect to undergo a cardiac surgery to fix my heart for the sake of preparing me for the next season of my life.

What was clear to me at that time was the prompting to preach the Word of God, based on Philippians 2:13, which asserts the fact that God is constantly *"working in us to will and to act according to His good purpose."* It's God who works in us to change our lives for our own good and for the good of others.

On the other hand, we're expected to do our part continuing *"to work out our salvation with fear and trembling"* (Philippians 2:12). The process starts with our willingness to deal with our own issues, the internal pains and struggles that rob us of the joy of living in intimacy and relationship with God and with others in our life. It starts with us; we must do our part if we want God to do His part.

The result is an increasing willingness to change as God directs, like going through a series of renewal and transformation; refining not only the mind but our body, soul and spirit.

To fulfill God's purpose requires not only an understanding of **who we are in Christ** but also who we should become as we continue to grow in faith. Choosing to align our will with His will as the Spirit brings revelation through the Word at various stages of our lives.

Jesus said, *"You are the salt of the earth… You are the light of the world"* (Matthew 5:13-14).

How can we be the salt of the earth if we lose sight of our usefulness, failing to do good whenever we can to our fellowmen, regardless of their status, skin colour, nationality or religion? How can we be the light of the world if the light of Christ does not shine within us with increasing brightness in places of darkness?

"Let your light shine before men, that they may see your good deeds and praise your Father in heaven" (Matthew 5:16) was what Jesus said to his followers.

RISING STAR OR DIMINISHING LIGHT

I see five stages, all beginning with the letter "S" that reflect our status, growing from one level of change to the next in God's redemption plan.

All of us, without exception, start at the same place as **Sinners** *"for all fall short of the glory of God…For the wages of sin is death, but the gift of God is eternal life in Christ Jesus our Lord."* (Romans 3:23, 6:23). Every man, woman or child has a choice to accept or reject God's gift of salvation to move from this starting position. To quote Billy Graham, "Our families cannot choose Christ for us. Our friends cannot do it. God is a great God, but even God can't make the decision for us…we have to make our own choice." [2]

The Bible tells us that through the redemption that came by Jesus as a sacrifice of atonement on the cross, those who

---

2. Franklin Graham, Billy Graham in Quotes, Thomas Nelson, Nashville, Tennessee, 2011

believe in Him through faith are spared sin's punishment—eternal separation from God. In other words, they become **Saints** the moment they repent of their sins and choose to confess Jesus Christ as their Saviour and Lord. Many church-goers seem happy to remain at this stage, thinking they have secured their ticket to heaven. I know this is true because I was one of them in my early years as a Christian. Lacking biblical knowledge and understanding, many do not see the need for further change even though there is so much more God has in store for them.

The next stage is revealed in the following Scripture, bringing us into a direct relationship with God the Father as **Sons**:

"For you did not receive a spirit that makes you a slave again to fear, but you received the Spirit of Sonship. And by Him we cry, 'Abba, Father.' The Spirit himself testifies with our spirit that we are God's children. Now if we are children, then we are heirs—heirs of God and co-heirs with Christ, if indeed we share in His sufferings in order that we may also share in His glory" (Romans 8:15-17).

We must never lose sight of our status as sons and daughters because this is what God desires above all—intimacy and relationship—being a Father who never cease to love His children with the promise of an inheritance in time to come.

I believe what brings forth a greater shine in our lives is when we choose to become **Servants** of Christ. As Jesus said, *"Whoever wants to become great among you must be your servant, and whoever wants to be the first must be your slave—just as the Son of man did not come to be served, but* *to serve, and to give his life as a ransom for many"* (Matthew 20:28). He set for us an example when He washed His disciples' feet (John 13:17). Are we willing to serve others out of love and obedience to Jesus? Sacrificial love which motivates us to serve others is what defines us as God's children. *"For God demonstrated His sacrificial love for us in that while we were still sinners, Christ died for us."* (Romans 5:8) A fruitful life is one that continues to do good works to others even when it's inconvenient to do so at times!

Finally, we will mature in status as **Soldiers** of Christ when we take up the call to contend against the forces of darkness overshadowing our land. The Bible says: *"For our struggle is not against flesh and blood, but against the rulers, against the authorities, against the powers of this dark world and against the spiritual forces of evil in the heavenly realms"* (Ephesians 6:12). Being alert, praying in the Spirit on all occasions with all kinds of prayers and requests, always keep on praying for all the saints, is what we're ordered to do as soldiers in God's army. We are to engage in the battle between light and darkness, good and evil. This is indeed a high calling because prayer, especially consistent intercessory prayer, is not what we would naturally do on a regular basis. Yet, Jesus told his disciples in a parable of the persistent widow that they should always pray and not give up (Luke 18:1-8).

It's time to move up with the changing season. We need change to bring a greater sense of purpose and fruitfulness in our lives; a greater measure of righteousness governing our lives from the inside out. In a world in which we are seeing increasing strife and conflict around us, we need changes that will bring people and families together so that we can live in love and relationship, peace and harmony with each other according to God's original plan for mankind.

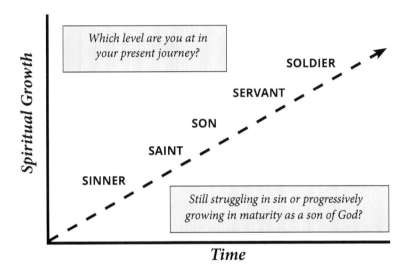

CHAPTER 3

HOPE IN PLACE OF HOPELESSNESS

There are times in our journey when life throws a curve at us. It can come suddenly and unexpectedly to upset our balance, causing us to fall. Sometimes it's beyond our ability to cope. We need help but who can we turn to? Who could truly understand and deliver us from our internal struggles and pain? We may feel like giving up but giving up is not an option because life is about living to overcome, not dying in shame and defeat. We must resolve to be overcomers for there will be better days ahead!

After finishing high school, I had just started work with Straits Times, a major newspaper publishing company, when my world was turned upside down due to the sudden death of my father at the age of 47. He was the sole breadwinner. A painting contractor by trade, he had little savings and left us with nothing to pay the bills.

"What am I going to do?"

I was overwhelmed by the sense of responsibility. I felt the heavy burden to take over my father's place having to provide and look after my mother and younger sister. The more I thought about my situation, the more desperate and hopeless I felt as a young man who didn't see any future in my life. There were days when the thought of death came creeping into my mind.

In my early years, growing up in the home of my grandparents, I simply went along with whatever gods they worshipped, either in temples or on the family altar. However, I could not relate with any of them even though I could see how fervently my grandmother worshipped them on her knees every morning, praying to some unknown god above.

Strangely enough, I was on the verge of total despair when I felt prompted to seek the meaning of life. I first visited a Catholic church, called Novena, where devotees were urged to attend at least seven Saturdays in order to have their prayers answered. That didn't work for me even though I went for nine Saturdays in a row. I went to a Lutheran church the following week but didn't feel any difference either. Later, I was brought to a Pentecostal church by a friend but didn't quite fit in because the young people were speaking in an unknown tongue when they prayed together in a group.

Finally, I found myself in a Methodist church where I quietly slipped in on a Sunday. I was hoping that no one would notice me because I thought no one would understand what I was going through. At the end of the service, an elderly gentleman who sat beside me extended his hand and simply greeted me with a friendly smile and a gentle voice.

"Hi, my name is Ng Kwok Hee. Welcome."

The following Sunday, I slipped into the same church during the service and was intending to leave as soon it was over. Guess who happened to sit beside me? Ng Kwok Hee, the same gentleman, who greeted me last Sunday.

I'm forever grateful to Mr. Ng because it was through his love and encouragement that I found myself in church Sunday after Sunday…until I was finally convinced that I needed a Saviour and was baptized as a believer of Jesus Christ on an Easter Sunday at Faith Methodist Church in Singapore.

A NEW LIFE OF HOPE AND PURPOSE

The Bible clearly tells us, *"For God so loved the world that He gave his one and only Son, that whoever believes in Him shall not perish but have eternal life"* (John 3:16). Receiving God's love and gift of salvation was the **biggest** turning point in my life! As Jesus said, *"I have come that they may have life, and have it to the full"* (John 10:10). Indeed, I was given a new lease of life; a purpose for living. Where previously there was hopelessness, there was now a sense of hope. Where previously I was all alone with no one to turn to for help, there was now a church family that I could lean on for encouragement and support in my journey of faith. I thank God for saving me and turning my life around so that I could face the future with confidence and hope. It was a confidence based on what God said about my new-found status as a son of God and hope based on what God promised in His Word:

"How great is the love the Father has lavished on us, that we should be called children of God! And that's what we are!" (1 John 3:1)

"His divine power has given us everything we need for life and godliness through our knowledge of him who called us by his own glory and goodness. Through these he has given us his very great and precious promises, so that through them you may participate in the divine nature and escape the corruption in the world caused by evil desires" (2 Peter 1:3-4).

Things were moving forward as I gradually learned to read the Bible and apply the principles that would govern my life, enabling me to grow as a Christian and later to serve in various leadership positions in the church. At my workplace in the newspaper publishing company, I was also making progress; moving from one department to another after earning a diploma from the U.K. Institute of Advertising and a Certificate in Management from the Singapore Institute of Management.

FINDING MY SWEETHEART

Catherine also worked in the same company and her office was next to where my desk was situated. We were separated by a glass panel, she on the inside and I on the outside. We became friends when we were involved in helping a female colleague of hers who was having some trouble with her father at home. Accompanying this troubled colleague home from time to time gave us the opportunity to spend some evenings together enabling us to get acquainted with each other.

Even after she left to work for an American refinery with a better paying job, our friendship grew stronger with time. We would walk for miles along the harbour-front at Queen Elizabeth Walk whenever I accompanied her home after work on her twice-weekly visit at my place. We had lots to talk about and felt drawn to each other even though, at the back of my mind, I had some reservation about our long-term relationship.

What was my reservation? The gap that was evident in our family background. While her father was a businessman who ran a profitable family business, my father was an uneducated contractor who could hardly make ends meet each month. How could I provide her a good life given my meagre income at that time?

One evening, I told her plainly that she would be better off with someone from the same station of life as her business class family. I was prepared to break off our friendship for her sake but she wouldn't hear of it. So we stuck it out for the next four years, happily spending time together, mostly walking along the harbour-front on the way to her home after her visit at my place.

One day, her mother said to me, "You two have been together for almost five years. Isn't it time to get engaged and plan for marriage?" That immediately set in motion our engagement followed by our wedding on December 20, 1969. This was certainly a major turning point for me; I finally felt accepted as a member of her family. I was 25 then, she was 22. By God's grace, life seemed to be getting better and better. Not only did I now have a wife and a love companion but I was blessed with increasing opportunities for personal growth and advancement both at work and church.

A JOB CHANGE WITH BIG RISK

In early 1970, I took a bold step in leaving The Straits Times to join a start-up newspaper called Singapore Herald. It was a big risk considering the odds against it. Not only was it pitted against the biggest competitor, The Straits Times, a long-established English newspaper in the nation, Singapore Herald had a small editorial staff and was funded primarily by a foreign investor. However, it had big aspirations to be a "second voice" for the English-speaking public, to boldly express its opinions even if they should conflict with the policies of the Singapore government.

I took the job because the offer came through its managing director and I was looking for a career change at that time. I was very impressed with Jimmy H. during the interview because he was such a good communicator with his kind and warm personality. When he expressed his confidence in me by offering me the position of Advertising & Sales Promotion Executive, I was ready to get on board.

It was a real challenge for me to go out and seek prospective clients in the early days, given their preference to advertise in The Straits Times and the fact that I had little sales experience. As time went on, however, I discovered that smaller companies were sympathetic to our cause and were more willing to lend their support by advertising in the new newspaper on a trial basis. When one company's advertisement appeared, it was exciting for me to see other companies coming on board—one by one—in order to keep up with the competition.

Unfortunately, the good times lasted only a few months after the Singapore Herald appeared on the news-stands. It was having problems with its news and editorial comments. Being openly critical of government policies and restrictions was a bold stand but it brought a backlash that became a threat to its survival. Its future was uncertain and I could see rising tension in the office.

One day, a call came through. Much to my surprise, it was from my former boss, the Group Personnel Manager in Straits Times. He asked me how things were at my workplace and whether I was interested in returning to fill a new position in one of the subsidiary companies. Times Printers was seeking a Personnel and Administration Manager and he was prepared to offer me the appointment with the salary I asked for over the phone.

I felt uneasy over the thought of abandoning ship at that stage. However, I found a chance to speak to Jimmy H. When I mentioned the job offer from Straits Times, he spoke kindly to me like a mentor blessing me to accept it and leave as soon as I could.

Looking back, this was another turning point in my journey. Within less than a year Singapore Herald was forced to shut down because its printing permit was revoked by the Singaporean government.

CHAPTER 4

A NEW PHASE OF CHANGE

Our journey can sometimes take us to unexpected places where we could be tested and stretched in order to prepare us to launch into the next phase of life—one that offers new opportunities for us to grow and even prosper individually and as a family. We need to be open to such seasons of change even when things seem difficult and the pressures overwhelming. There are no guarantees in life. You do what you can with whatever you have, and chances are that you will have a break to change your course for a brighter future.

Our decision to migrate to Canada was made as a New Year resolution. We had prayed to God to open the door if it was His will for us to move to Toronto where Susan, my sister-in-law, lived. She was the one who encouraged us and sponsored our application. When the visa came through within six months, we were certain that it was God's plan for us to be in Canada and there was no hesitation whatsoever in making the move in August 1976.

By that time, we had been married for almost seven years and had two sons, aged five and two-and-a-half. I had risen in position as a Personnel and Administration Manager with the newspaper publishing company but was prepared to give it up for the sake of seeking a better future for our kids.

However, coming to Canada as an immigrant meant starting life all over again with finding a job and a home to settle down. It was a huge challenge for me as the head of the family to adapt to the new reality that we would have to stay with Susan until such time that we could afford to move out and set up our own home. As a nurse who had to work night shifts, Susan had to sleep during the day and this put a heavy constraint on our two boys. They had to be told again and again not to make too much noise while they were playing at home.

MY FIRST JOB IN CANADA

I'll never forget the first job I took a few weeks after we arrived. It was a factory position advertised in the Toronto Sun. I was eager to gain Canadian experience and was prepared to accept any job. Even so, I was surprised that the boss would hire me on the spot after only a brief interview. I was to report for work the next day. The pay was $3.25 an hour.

This was a small lampshade company that had about fifteen workers. When I reported for work the next day, the boss introduced me to an eighteen-year-old operator, whose job was to cut thick stacks of plastic sheets with a band saw, following a template tracing the shape of a lampshade. I was to watch and learn on the job.

A NEW PHASE OF CHANGE

Working in an office all along in Singapore and not having any mechanical experience, I was fearful of the ear-splitting noise every time the band saw cut through each stack of plastic sheets. At the end of the day, I was told that the eighteen-year-old operator had quit the same day and I was to take over as the operator. You can imagine how fearful I felt that evening, thinking about the band saw and how dangerous it could be if a mishap should happen on the job. I was breaking out in cold sweat during the night.

However, I reported for duty the next morning and was able to complete the shift, hiding my fears while manoeuvring each stack of plastic sheets over the band saw table. On the third day, while I was cutting a stack, the band saw suddenly broke loose and was spinning over and over inside the housing above. I nearly jumped out of my skin with fright. Needless to say, I was again sweating it out in bed that night, keeping the fear to myself so as not to disturb the family.

I dutifully reported for work the next day. In the afternoon, the boss appeared on the factory floor. I had noticed whenever he was around, he usually had his right hand in the pocket of his trousers. That day, for whatever reason, he took it out and I saw a stump instead of a hand.

Did he lose his hand on the band saw? Putting two and two together, I could see the risk of losing my hand and so I decided on the spot that I would quit the next day. When I informed the boss of my decision, he commended me for being a good worker and persuaded me not to leave. He even offered to train me as a foreman if I would stay.

However, I was glad to leave this fearful episode and start all over again in search of another job.

FIRST SIX MONTHS

Facing the pressure to provide for my family, I took whatever job that came along even though most were low-paying, hourly-rated factory jobs. Within the first six months, I had switched jobs with 5 different companies; even trying to sell vacuum cleaners by appointment in the homes on a commission basis. I was going nowhere. The feeling of regret deep within me was growing every time I thought about the prestigious job I had left behind as a Personnel Manager in my spacious and comfortable office in Singapore. I felt I was going through the same nightmare every day. Nevertheless, I was determined to tough it out.

"No turning back," I said to myself. "No turning back."

Through Molly, my younger sister-in-law who was serving as a missionary with Overseas Missionary Fellowship, we were introduced to a Brethren church, Bridlegrove Bible Chapel, in Scarborough where we became members for a number of years. It was the first place where we were socially exposed to a foreign culture; a Canadian church to help our family better integrate into the Canadian society. However, I found that unlike the Chinese who tend to be quiet and reserved, the Canadians were more open and talkative even to strangers. It was embarrassing to have someone in church asked me from time to time, "What do you do?" or "Where do you work?"

Surprisingly, I was approached within a short period of

time by an Elder, asking if I would consider serving as a Deacon in the church. He apparently saw the potential in me even though I didn't see it in myself. Not having a decent job at that time I felt unworthy. So I resisted the invitation. Even though we were receiving sound biblical teaching and good Christian fellowship in the church, I was disinterested in any form of service, much less an official position as a Deacon.

One day, for whatever reason I could not recall, I decided to say 'Yes' when I was again approached to become a Deacon, this time by another Elder. I accepted the responsibility to take on the treasurer's position, even though I had no knowledge or experience in accounting. However, with Catherine's help, I was able to carry out all the necessary treasury functions including the financial and budget presentations required at annual general meetings for the next three years.

FIRST BREAKTHROUGH

Looking back, it was strange to see the events unfolding following my decision to accept the deaconship position at Bridlegrove Bible Chapel. It seemed God was waiting for me to get out of my shell to start serving Him through His church. It was as if He was withholding His hand to give me the break I needed to get a proper job.

Through Canada Manpower, I was given an interview at Thomas Nelson Book Publishing where I landed my first office job as a production assistant. What took place at the interview was most unusual and surprising. Looking at my application form, the Director said he would hire me but not at the salary I had asked for. It was too low, he said. I gladly went along with the higher salary he proposed and was hired on the same day. Praise be to God for His favour and provision!

Six months later, with the savings we had brought, together with some funds withdrawn from a Pension Plan in Singapore called the Central Provident Fund , we were able to put a down payment to purchase our first home in Scarborough. However, we had to give up our Singapore citizenship as a requirement to pull out our funds before the retirement age of 55. By doing so, we had resolved to settle in Canada as our home country.

"No turning back," I said to myself. "No turning back."

Moving into our new home after we had stayed with Susan for just over a year was another early breakthrough, allowing us to enjoy the freedom of our own space as a young family.

In the early years, Catherine had to seek a part-time job to supplement our family income. However, with two young sons at home, she could not have a regular day-time job while I was at work. As she prayed, it wasn't long before a door was opened at Med-Chem Lab, a medical laboratory, for her to work part-time in the evening in an office job. It was an arrangement that worked well for us because she would leave after dinner, and return home before midnight, working five days a week. When the children were old enough to switch to a full-day class, she was able to adjust her part-time hours (from 10 a.m. to 2 p.m.) and be at home before the end of the school-day.

MORE BREAKTHROUGHS AT WORK

At Thomas Nelson, I was promoted to the position of Company Services Supervisor within a year and enjoyed a close working relationship with Kevin N, the Director who hired me. He was a demanding executive who took pride in his position as Production Director of a major book publishing company. It was a privilege to gain his confidence and there were days he would invite me out for lunch, sharing with me his background and the pressure he was facing at work.

Apparently, he had been raised as an orphan by an aunt in England and this might have been a factor why he was such a perfectionist, expecting and even demanding the best from his office staff. At one time, he confided in me that his doctor had advised him to slow down for the sake of his health because he was "burning his candle at both ends."

Working at Thomas Nelson gave me the opportunity to learn about printing and the book publishing business, steering me in a different direction from my personnel administration background. God was preparing me for what was to come. Looking back, it was interesting to see how this plan was fulfilled over a period of around 13 years before I launched my own graphic arts and sales promotion business called Dynacom Graphics Inc.

STEPPING STONES

These were the stepping stones that enabled me to learn and be equipped to run my own graphic arts, printing and sales promotion business which started in 1990. From Thomas Nelson I moved to Hunter Rose, a company that specialized in the printing and binding of books. This move was prompted by a job offer that came from an ex-colleague at Thomas Nelson after the Production Director suddenly passed away.

From Hunter Rose, I made another move to Maclean Hunter Publishing where I worked as a Senior Production Co-ordinator. My task was to oversee a department responsible for the printing of several weekly and monthly magazines.

From Maclean Hunter, I made one more move to Gaylord Planned Promotion. With this company I was able to learn the sales promotion business. I was initially the assistant to the top salesman. Later I became an account manager, selling the company's promotional services to selected clients in the city of Toronto.

God had been preparing the way all along. I know this to be true because I didn't apply to work for any of these companies. Strange as it seemed, I was approached by recruiters to consider the job opening available in each of these three companies. How they got my name remained a mystery to me. But the result was clearly beneficial. With each change of job, I saw an increase in my monthly income. More importantly, each job was also imparting to me a deeper knowledge and understanding of the printing and sales promotion business.

CHAPTER 5

VENTURE INTO BUSINESS

In our journey of life, we realize that there are no shortcuts or easy paths to take us where we want to go. Success does not come without effort, discipline and perseverance. While it's true that everyone has an innate desire to succeed in life, we must also be realistic about our goals and be prepared to face failures whenever they come. As Winston Churchill once said, "Success is not final, failure is not fatal: It is the courage to continue that counts." However, there are times we see opportunity knocking at our door, when it takes real courage to accept the risks and change direction even when we are uncertain whether the road is leading us to success or failure ahead.

As I mentioned earlier, at Gaylord Planned Promotion, I had the privilege to work under Duncan M, the top salesman, as his assistant. In view of my dedication, doing whatever it took to get the job done, I was able to gain his confidence over a period of about three years. Even though we had the staff to handle every aspect of each promotional project, I gradually took it upon myself to be involved in the creative and production process by interacting with the art director and the foremen of the film and printing departments and with the paper and display suppliers. In other words, I was given the liberty to manage each project hands on, even dealing with clients whenever there was a need to do so.

I was well regarded in the company given my work performance and ability to relate with people. As much as I enjoyed my work, however, I could see that the people who were making a lot of money were the salesmen who were paid on commission based on the revenue they brought in for each project. Not only were they well-paid, they had the liberty to determine their own working hours as account managers.

I thought to myself, "I should get into sales and be an account manager."

I brought up the matter with John D, the president and co-owner of the company. However, he told me that I would need to have either a MBA (Master in Business Administration degree) or have managed at least $1 million in business volume to qualify as an account manager. John D was a quiet but forceful gentleman; I knew he meant what he said. In spite of this, I managed to convey to him my strong desire to get into sales and would look for such opportunities either within Gaylord or somewhere else.

It wasn't long before he sent his Vice President to speak to me. During lunchtime, he grilled me to see how serious my intention was to leave Gaylord if I was able to find a sales job elsewhere. I made it clear to him that I would pursue this goal however long it took. Soon after, I had another meeting with John D and to my surprise he made me an offer to be a sales trainee with the prospect of being appointed as an account manager within a year. This was my first breakthrough into sales—a turning point which set in motion some very significant changes and improvements to my life.

My first opportunity came through a Dale Carnegie public-speaking course, which the company partially paid for me. This was clearly a life-changing experience for me because it helped me to overcome my lack of confidence and fear of men. I was given a real boost in confidence when, against all the other good speakers in the class, I was voted one evening as the winner of the Impromptu Speaking Contest.

My second opportunity was through going out and interacting directly with clients and potential clients. I was gaining confidence in meeting people at different levels, cultivating relationships while bringing in more and more business along the way.

I still remember a private meeting I had one day with John D soon after my appointment as a sales trainee. As I mentioned earlier, he was a quiet but forceful gentleman. I could see that he was a man of stature and a well-respected president of the company. However, when he spoke about his background, I was surprised that he was also the top salesman for many years. He didn't have a flamboyant personality like I saw in most successful sales people; his demeanor was more like a soft-spoken diplomat.

What was the secret of his success? Relationship was the key, he said; taking time to build relationship and trust with customers beyond the normal course of doing business. This was an unexpected piece of advice that I kept in my heart, and it certainly served me well in terms of my success as a salesperson and subsequently as a business owner after I left Gaylord.

HOW OUR BUSINESS STARTED

Jerry A. was the major partner who owned Gaylord Planned Promotion. He was looking forward to his upcoming retirement at 65. However, we were told before he reached his birthday that he was ill. A few days later, the sad news came that he had suddenly passed away.

We were all shocked by the news, given the fact he was like the backbone of Gaylord. He started the business many years ago with John D who remained a junior partner. The future of the company was at stake; the writings were on the wall for those who could see its precarious state in those days.

It was in the midst of this uncertain period that I witnessed again the intervention of God's hand while I was at a loss what to do. Strangely enough, calls from recruiters started coming in even though I hadn't started looking for employment elsewhere. My interview with two companies resulted in two offers, both in sales. One was with a major printing company in the Don Mills area and the other was with a privately owned company specializing in promotional displays.

There was an interesting twist in the second offer from the owner of the company. When I met him for the first time, I was very impressed with his sincerity, openly sharing with me about his early years in Canada, arriving as an immigrant from England with only two bags. Starting from scratch, he was able to start his own business and now owned several businesses in Toronto. He was currently looking at hiring someone reliable to expand the company's operations. After several meetings held in classy restaurants over lunch and dinner, he took me to see one of his factories where promotional displays were being produced. I stated my terms, including a Volvo company car. He agreed and I was ecstatic since I had never been treated with such favour before. However, he later dropped the bombshell, saying he needed his junior partner's agreement for my appointment. A meeting was arranged. A few days later he called and gave me the disappointing news.

"Sorry, I can't proceed with your appointment because I don't have the agreement of my partner."

I must admit that I was fretting for a while, questioning why God would let this happen to me, allowing me to go through first the high, and then the low point. However, He had a better plan that was revealed to me shortly after that disappointing experience. Out of the blue, my client at Christie Brown & Company said to me one day:

"Why don't you step out and run your own business? My boss and I will support you."

A client who became a friend over time, Peter M, was aware

of what was happening at Gaylord. Having dealt with me for several years, he could see the potential in me to service his needs but at a lower cost. With his encouragement and assurance that I could continue to service the account, specializing in the quarterly production of a Christie Profit Planner for its national sales force, I took the plunge and started Dynacom Graphics Inc. after resigning from Gaylord in 1990.

Running our own business was the most satisfying and financially rewarding period of our working life for both Catherine and me. Christie Brown & Company was our major customer and we were kept busy by servicing that account alone with some other work coming occasionally from a few minor clients. This went on for a number of years, allowing us to consolidate our position as a preferred supplier to Christie Brown, given the relationships we were able to build with many of its product managers over time.

However, like any business that faced changes in the marketplace, we also faced the threat of losing our major account. There was a report that Kraft Canada would be taking over Nabisco Inc., which owned the operations of Christie Brown. I could see the hand-writing on the wall.

ONE DOOR SHUTS, THREE DOORS OPEN

While I was working at Gaylord, Catherine and I had decided to take a family trip back to Singapore. We had been away from our birthplace for almost 14 years. As mentioned earlier, the company had been shaken by the sudden death of Jerry A, the major partner. Should we still go ahead with this expensive vacation, looking at the uncertainty and turmoil at Gaylord? Nevertheless, we took a one-month vacation, trusting God to take care of whatever was to come. And He did by directing our steps in starting Dynacom Graphics Inc.!

This time, facing the prospect of losing Christie Brown, Catherine and I were again considering whether we should take a planned vacation to go to Israel. We decided to go anyway, again trusting God to take care of whatever was to come.

Shortly after, in conversation with Carolyn H, a product manager at Christie Brown, I was surprised when she told me that she too was going to Israel around the same time we had booked our tour. We agreed to meet in Israel.

We were quite transparent with each other when we met and had dinner one evening in the hotel near Jerusalem where we were staying. When I confided to her about my desire to serve God when I retire, she confided to me that she had returned to Israel to find her root. She said that she belonged to a small Jewish sect and wanted to learn its language so she could teach the children and preserve its language and culture. I was very impressed by her willingness to give up her marketing job along with her MBA qualification to follow her dream. That meeting turned out to be a harbinger of better things to come a year later!

One day, I received a phone call from Carolyn. I asked her whether she was calling from Israel and was surprised when she told me that she had returned to Toronto. Apparently, she had run out of funds and had to return to build up her savings again. I offered to buy her lunch. A few weeks later, she called again and told me that she had left her job with a Jewish synagogue and was now working with Dixie, a manufacturer of paper cups and plates. This company was interested in a sales profit planner, like the one we produced for Christie Brown. Carolyn was calling to introduce me to the Marketing Director of Dixie. It was the first door that opened the way for us to expand our business while facing the loss of Christie Brown due to the Kraft takeover.

Dixie turned out to be a really good account even though our sales revenue was about a quarter of Christie Brown's. When Carolyn's temporary contract ended, she introduced me to Colleen D, another product manager who took over her job at Dixie. Colleen worked for a couple of months with me on the project before she decided to leave for Heinz Canada. Through this contact, Colleen brought me to Heinz a few months later. This was the second door that was opened for us to develop more new business, resulting in a steady flow of promotional material that Heinz required for its on-going in-store couponing program.

A third door was opened when, out of the blue, I received a phone call from Reena L, a former product manager of Christie Brown, inviting me to meet her at Nestlé Canada. She was keen to create a profit planner for its sales force as part of a new initiative to have a greater merchandising presence in the stores. We were able to produce the creative work she was expecting. As a result, another profitable account came quite unexpectedly after we were completely cut off by Kraft's preferred supplier policy.

Even though we were a small company, we had connections with some major clients, such as Christie Brown, Dixie, Heinz and Nestlé. They kept us busy for 14 years, running the business with increasing earnings and savings until I decided to retire at the age of 60.

CHAPTER 6

CHANGING PACE

We have to pace ourselves in our journey, recognizing the need to slow down when it's time to rest. The Bible tells us *"There is a time for everything, and a season for every activity under heaven."* (Ecclesiastes 3:1) Accept this or not, there is a time to work and a time to retire. In today's rapidly changing economy, there is no guarantee of job security no matter how long we've worked for a company. As we have seen time and time again, a business that is regarded as a darling in the investment market today may turn out to be a dud, should the tide turn and force it to shut down. In such times of uncertainty, we must be watchful and prepared to change pace. Saving as much as we can is a prudent goal, not only to prepare for the rainy days in case of a job loss but also to pave the way toward retirement.

God had a plan for my retirement and He made it evidently clear when I celebrated my 60th birthday with my family and some members of the church at the Mandarin Buffet Restaurant. That evening, someone brought a bunch of helium-filled balloons imprinted with the figure 60 on them. My immediate thought was to distribute all the balloons to my grandkids.

However, a guest brought me one of the balloons and said, "This is yours, take it home." So I took the balloon home and left it hanging on the ceiling of my office that evening.

The next morning, as I was looking at the balloon still hanging at the ceiling, I distinctly heard a voice that said, "Let it go."

I immediately took it outside and standing at the balcony of our pent-house, I said this short prayer before letting the balloon loose: "Lord, you've been a faithful God who has taken care of me and my family for the last 60 years. Today, I release my life to serve you in whatever way you lead."

It was a 'dangerous' prayer because God took my words seriously and started stripping me of all of our business accounts until there was none left within a period of six months. Deep inside, I knew it was time to retire and there was a sense of peace and acceptance, given the fact that my clients were also moving on due to personal reasons or reorganizational changes at their workplace.

As for the balloon, it ascended into the clear blue sky, carried by a strong wind that sent it drifting eastward until it was out of sight within a couple of minutes.

Why am I sharing my story with such detailed accounts of the circumstances that had changed and shaped my life in good times and in bad times? It is because I am compelled to share my personal journey as a testimony in order to give God all the glory for all that He has done in my life. I could not have done all the things I did without His grace and help. Had He not reached down to save and deliver me from the pit of hopelessness when I was 21, I would have been lost. Through His love, peace and joy, He has enabled me to press on throughout my journey as a believer, including my position as a pastor in a local church called Toronto Life-Spring Christian Fellowship.

Today, as we look at our children and grandchildren, our hearts are filled with thanksgiving to God for the way He has blessed us as a family. A chartered accountant by profession, our older son Joo-Lip works as the Director of Finance in the Canadian branch of an international biotech company based in California; he and his wife, Lynnette, have eight children. A doctor and a specialist in internal medicine, our younger son Joo-Meng works with Trillium Health Centre; he and his wife, Rosanna, have four children. We can be justly proud of our sons and daughters-in-law not only because they have achieved so much more in terms of their education and careers, but also because of the way they are raising their children with Christ as the center of their family. Above everything else, our prayer is that they and their children would be the godly off-springs who will love and honour God, keeping alive our family motto: *"As for me and my household, we will serve the Lord"* (Joshua 24:15).

A HOUSE IS MORE THAN A HOME

On the home front, it was interesting to see in hindsight how God was directing my steps in upgrading our house through the years. Our first home was a 1,100 square feet, three-bedroom townhouse which we bought in

Scarborough in 1977. We were quite happy with this house and would have stayed in it for the rest of our lives, had it not been for a word given to me quite unexpectedly by a client. Peter M. put a seed thought in my head by saying, "You should look at your house not just as a home but an investment." He encouraged me to consider selling and buying our house when the market conditions were favourable for such investment decisions to be made.

He was right!

After staying in our townhouse for ten years—by which time it had appreciated in price by almost 100 percent—we sold it and bought a 2,000 square feet, four-bedroom detached home.

We spent five years in this second home, still living in Scarborough, and would have stayed on had it not been for another word that came prompting me to look at a new section in Brampton called Springdale. We were together on the airplane flying back to Singapore when John Tan, our pastor, informed me that he was planning to purchase a bigger house in that new development.

On my return, I decided to check it out on a Saturday. I invited my sister-in-law, Susan, to come along. It was another strange but exciting day in my journey.

As we set out in the morning the rain came and was pouring down heavier and heavier like cats and dogs as the saying goes. As we exited from the highway, we took a left turn trying to find our direction in the heavy rain that had affected our visibility. Somehow, I sensed it was a wrong turn and decided to turn back heading east instead of going westward. As we approached the sales office some three miles away I said to Susan, "I have a strong feeling that the rain will stop when we arrive at the site."

And when we stepped out of the car in the parking area, there wasn't a single drop when we walked into the sales office. Given this clear sign from heaven, both Susan and I decided on that day to put in our offer for two houses which a year later became our homes for the next ten years in Brampton. Both of us bought the same model, a spacious two-storey 3,300 square feet detached house with five-bedrooms in it!

In 2002, we made our next move, downsizing to a two-bedroom penthouse since our two sons had married and were no longer living with us. We enjoyed the view and comfort of living in this new home, and because it was managed as a condominium community, there were more opportunities in the next ten years for us to lock up the place and travel to many distant places whenever we could take a break from the business and go on vacation.

Looking back, every move that we made was timely. Each house had greatly appreciated in value with the rising real estate market over the last three decades. Had we stay put in our first townhouse, we would not have been able to build as much equity as we now have, given the lower cost we paid for our present bungalow.

CHAPTER 7

BIRTHING A NEW CHURCH

Just as every person needs a family, I believe every new immigrant needs a community to help support one another. The truth is that man was not designed to live in isolation but in a loving relationship with God and men. Both our physical and spiritual needs are met when this relationship is intact. This caused us to live not independently but interdependently in community with others. It's hard to imagine how difficult life would be if circumstances were to cause a breakdown in relationship, leaving a man or woman separated from his or her family. A person would be alone to cope with his or her pains and wounds. I discovered that the church is one place where broken lives can be redeemed and restored. Where people can experience love and relationship with one another like a family.

Who could have thought that we would be involved in starting a church in our early years as immigrants in Toronto? Apart from the church family at Bridlegrove Bible Chapel, we had a limited circle of people we knew mainly through my sister-in-law Susan. Yet, God worked in mysterious ways to make the necessary connections to gather a core group in order to start a church.

This was how it all started. When Molly, my sister-in-law, came to Toronto in the late 1970s, she was looking for someone from Singapore to befriend. She looked through the telephone directory and found a Chinese name—Maisie Tan—whom she contacted and later met. It turned out that Maisie also came from Singapore. In fact, it was through her that a Bible study group was subsequently started in her home.

What brought the core group together was a wedding which took place in 1978. Maisie's sister, Angela, came to Canada as an immigrant and a wedding was planned two weeks after her fiancé, Eric Wee, arrived in Toronto. We were invited to attend the wedding together with Maisie's Christian friends who were also from Singapore. This was how the group met and came to know each other for the first time.

A seed was sown at one of the Bible study sessions when someone said, "Why don't we look into starting a church for Malaysians and Singaporeans since there is a need for these immigrants, especially students who are studying in the colleges and universities in Toronto and in need of family support?"

What followed was a series of meetings and steps that finally led to the formation of the Malaysian-Singaporean Bible Church (MSBC), which was birthed on April 5, 1981. We had prayed to God for a central location, accessible by subway for anyone—especially university students from Malaysia/Singapore—who didn't have their own means of transportation. And God provided by opening the door to a Salvation Army church located at Yonge & Eglinton where the church was first planted.

At that time I was still serving as an Elder at Bridlegrove Bible Chapel. We were somewhat torn between serving in both churches, one in the morning and the other in the afternoon. For a period of time, we attended both churches with our two young sons until I sensed the call to give up one of them in order to commit myself fully to the other. Thus, I resigned my elder position at Bridlegrove and committed fully to MSBC. As one of the founders that started MSBC, it proved to be a step in the right direction. This was where I found the greatest joy in my service to God and His people.

As the number increased in MSBC over the years, several moves were made to relocate the church. Interestingly, all of them were along the central corridor of Yonge Street, close to its subway line and in answer to our prayer!

First move: Central Gospel Hall at Yonge and Bloor (1982 – 1990);

Second move: Bedford Park Church at Yonge and Lawrence (1990 – 2000);

Third move: Willowdale Pentecostal Church at Yonge and Finch (2000 – present time).

In answer to our prayer, all of them were accessible by subway!

PASTORAL LEADERSHIP

We needed pastoral leadership and God was faithful in sending pastors to step in at the right time. Dr. William Wan, a pastor in Ottawa, served as our theological advisor in the beginning from April 1981 to December 1983. Next came Dr. Siang-Yang Tan, a professor of psychology and counseling at Ontario Bible College (now known as Tyndale University) in Toronto, who served as our first pastor on a part-time basis from April 1984 to July 1985. As the church grew in number, we saw the need to have a full-time pastor. Faithful as always, God sent Pastor John Tan all the way from Singapore to take up his first pastorate, which he faithfully served from January 1986 to August 2003. Alvin Koh was appointed as an Assistant Pastor in July 1996 and became the Lead Pastor in September 2003 when MSBC went through a period of transition after a church split.

Duncan Westwood and Victor Koh (Associate Pastors) and Adrian Wi (Youth Pastor) also served in the pastoral team prior to August 2003. Thomas Chong served as an Associate Pastor from 2005 to 2008 after the church split. Adrian Wi was subsequently appointed as an Associate Pastor when he returned to Toronto in 2007.

THE EARLY YEARS

Like a plant growing over time, MSBC was drawing more and more newcomers into the church. We had good worship, good food and fellowship with good programs to meet the needs of both the young and old.

We wanted to see people building relationship with one another beyond the regular Sunday gathering, so small groups were encouraged to meet in homes for fellowship and bible study during the week. Embracing the vision "To be a Total Cell Church" by year 2000, cell groups were taught to focus on the 4Ws in order to have a well-rounded program to grow their faith whenever they met on a bi-weekly basis. The 4Ws were: Welcome, Worship, Word and Works.

MSBC was an active church that seemed to be doing well with the programs it was running for the people. We had FAM (Family Adult Ministry), catering to adults and families. We had YAM (Young Adult Ministry), catering to college/university students and young working adults. And of course, we had a Sunday School for the children.

While there was a desire to reach out to people regardless of their race or nationality, the name of the church appeared to be a hindrance for many who came and try to fit into our Malaysian-Singaporean culture.

"Why not change the name and remove a label that discourages others from joining the church?"

This was a question that was raised time and time again. However, given the resistance by the majority, the name was kept and the result was a close-knit community of mostly Malaysians and Singaporeans meeting at MSBC.

We were planning to purchase a church building at Bedford Park in 1990. It was vacant at the time and we were told that at least two parties were bidding for the property.

"How much should we bid if we're really interested, given its location steps away from the subway station?"

One leader proposed $633,000 based on Matthew 6:33, *"But seek first his kingdom and his righteousness and all these things will be given to you as well."* However, the rest of the leadership felt it would be safer to go with a higher bid at $650,000. After the offer was made and accepted, we were pleasantly surprised to receive a cheque for $60,000 from the trustees—which apparently showed that our bid was way too high, much more than the offers from the other parties. We thanked God for His goodness, covering what seemed like a weakness of faith on our part with this unexpected gift to reduce our mortgage debt-load.

By all appearance, it would be fair to say that we were doing well as a church in those days. There was a strong emphasis on the Word of God. In fact, several guest speakers even commended the church, expressing how strongly they felt the presence of God in our midst during worship. We had a growing membership and a committed team of Deacons to manage the administrative and financial affairs of the church. The church leaders were willing to work together in all decision-making matters. We avoided conflicts by not proceeding with any matter under discussion until everyone was on board after a period of waiting and praying. We had a clear vision to grow the church through cell groups by the year 2000.

BLIND SPOTS

Looking back, however, there were several "blind spots" that hindered our growth as a church. They only became apparent when we were going through a series of tests and crises in 1992 and 2002:

Blindspot #1—Lack of Unity: We thought we had a sound structure by forming groups, like FAM and YAM, in order to cater to the interests and needs of the different age groups. In reality, we were allowing group dynamics to separate or pull people together with the result that we had a church within a church. That became more apparent when our young people opted to have their own Sunday worship separate from the adult congregation. We didn't see it at the time but there was a gap growing between two generations; the result was that our young people were increasingly alienating themselves from the adults in the church. We were losing the next generation even as we believed in and spoke about the need for unity within the church.

Blindspot #2—Lack of Growth: While cell groups were encouraged to be open in receiving newcomers in order to grow and multiply, there was a lack of pastoral supervision to see this followed through. In reality, cell groups were free to do what they wanted—led either by a cell leader or by a few members taking turns in leading the group (choosing among themselves to study a selected book in the Bible or follow a DVD teaching on a recommended topic). As a result, people became more and more comfortable in their respective groups and were reluctant to move out of their comfort zone to mix and mingle with anyone outside their cell groups. There was little motivation to invite new people to join their bi-weekly meetings.

Blindspot #3—Lack of Transparency: The church was supposed to be a family where there would be mutual support and encouragement when someone was hurting or going through difficult times. In reality, even though people were familiar with each other within their cell groups, there was little open sharing about personal issues, partly because of cultural constraint and partly because of pride. For example, it's shameful in the Chinese culture to publicly reveal domestic problems even within a cell group; it would be better to keep the pain and struggle within the family than to "lose face" by asking for help. Eventually, even though the people were outwardly relating with each other in church, their relationships were found to be less than authentic when tested under the pressure of a crisis.

Blindspot #4—Lack of Outreach: The church clearly had a commission to *"go into all the world and preach the good news to all creation"* (Mark 16:15) and *"to make disciples of all nations"* (Matthew 28:19). Although the church had a policy to set aside at least ten percent of its annual income for supporting missionaries and mission organizations, there was little initiative and effort to teach and promote evangelism as a way to reach people with the gospel of Jesus Christ. In reality, we were quite content with the fact that we had sent two of our own missionaries into the mission field, gave towards the support of a few missionaries who were associated with the church, and contributed financially to a few mission organizations. We were expecting the people to come to the church instead of going out to reach them with the good news that could change their lives for good.

Blindspot #5—Lack of Spiritual Power: As a Bible church by name, we had a strong focus on the Word but there was little emphasis on the Spirit. In the Gospel of John, Jesus taught His disciples, *"And I will ask the Father, and he will give you another Counselor to be with you forever – the Spirit of truth"* (John 14:16-17), and *"But the Counselor, the Holy Spirit, whom the Father will send in my name, will teach you all things and will remind you of everything I have said to you"* (John 14:26). In reality, instead of constantly seeking the counsel of the Holy Spirit, the leaders were relying on the wisdom of men to manage the church and to make plans for its growth. However, like a bird flying with only one wing, the result was that we were more or less going in circles instead of soaring to where the church was called to be in order to carry out the mission of Jesus, which is to preach the kingdom of God, heal the sick and drive out demons. In my view, this was the most serious "blind spot" concerning the power and authority given by Jesus to the church to fulfill the Great Commission, apart from which there was no reason for its existence.

Blindspot #6—Lack of Intercessory Prayer: Although we often prayed whenever we met, there was a lack of emphasis on the importance of prayer. Yet Jesus taught that *"My house* (meaning the church) *will be called a house of prayer for all nations"* (Mark 11:17). There was a lack of intercession to pray for the church and the city, let alone the nations of the world. Instead of waiting on God to hear what He had in mind for us to pray and to intercede as prompted by the Holy Spirit, our prayers in those days were mostly focused on needs brought up by individuals.

It was not unusual for a cell group to have a prayer list of such items before they would start to pray at their regular meetings.

Blindspot #7—Lack of a Chosen Leader: While it was prudent to have a governing structure holding the Senior Pastor accountable to a Board of Elders, and vice versa, the principle behind the plurality of leadership did not work well in times when the church was tested in a crisis. What happened in 1992, and again in 2000, when the Holy Spirit suddenly came upon our people revealed how vulnerable the church could be when pastoral leadership was lacking in addressing the confusion following these two momentous events. In hindsight, we could see from the Scriptures that when God wanted to do something with his people, He called forth a man and gave him instructions, speaking directly into his spirit or indirectly through a vision or dream; nowhere did He call a committee or a board to meet and put His plans into action. We had an Executive Committee (EXCO) but no chosen leader with full authority to guide the flock at the time when the church was being shaken by the move of the Holy Spirit. The truth was that the church leaders didn't know better. Instead of inquiring with the Lord what was happening, we thought with our rational minds that it was best to let things simmer down. This was another "blind spot" that resulted in the church split in 2003, causing the majority of its members to leave in droves despite many years of fellowship with the remnant who chose to stay.

There is much work to be done to carry out the mission that Jesus left with his disciples before he departed to be with the Father in heaven:

"I tell you the truth, anyone who has faith in me will do what I have been doing. He will do even greater things than these, because I am going to the Father." (John 14:12)

This was a solemn word He gave to them before promising them the Holy Spirit who was to come and be their Counselor and Helper. What that work entails, which is clearly spiritual and beyond our human ability to fulfill apart from the enabling of the Holy Spirit, is summed up in these last words recorded in the Gospel of Mark:

"Go into all the world and preach the good news to all creation. Whoever believes and is baptized will be saved, but whoever does not believe will be condemned. And these signs will accompany those who believe; In my name they will drive out demons; they will speak in new tongues; they will pick up snakes with their hands; and when they drink deadly poison, it will not hurt them at all; they will place their hands on sick people, and they will be healed" (Mark 16:15-18).

This is what the church is called to do to demonstrate the power of God in redeeming mankind from their sins, sicknesses and bondages. Are we prepared to take up the call? It's encouraging to hear of churches that are open to this paradigm shift and are increasingly aligning with the Word of God to do what it says even though it's uncomfortable for many in the beginning.

In view of my active involvement from the beginning, since 1980 to the present time (2020), I felt it's incumbent on me to share some of the past events that have caused the church to change its course through the years to where it is today. Therefore, I will devote the rest of the book to continue the story of MSBC so others may see how God's hand has been guiding me and the church leaders in each season of its journey.

CHAPTER 8

SPIRITUAL REVIVAL

Just as there are turning points that cause changes in a person's life, there are seasons when unexpected events take place that can lead a church or institution to change its focus and direction. Their effect is best seen in retrospect by the end results.

In 1992, we had a spiritual revival when the Holy Spirit came upon the church and caused quite a number of people to fall or cry when they came forward in response to an altar call. We had never seen or experienced such an occurrence before. What happened was totally unexpected. While many were watching in wonder of what was going on, believing it to be the work of God, others were watching with skepticism, questioning if this was the work of the devil.

On the recommendation of Dr. Siang-Yang Tan, our first pastor, we had invited Dr. Joe Ozawa to come and speak to us over a weekend. Dr. Ozawa was a clinical psychologist from California who had a great passion to reach out to the poor and needy. He would spend much of his time and resources ministering to their needs. He was also a good communicator who preached the Word of God with power and conviction. Although he was simply speaking, teaching about the Holy Spirit from the Bible, many were rapt with attention over every word he said.

At the end of his message, he gave an invitation for people to come forward in response to God's call to step out and serve wherever He directed; even going out as missionaries if they were led to do so. Quite a number of our young adults moved forward. As Dr. Ozawa was praying for each of them, some fell down as if "slain" by the Spirit. Others were crying quietly as they stood, seemingly touched in their spirit.

Here are the testimonies from two individuals who were touched and whose lives have been deeply impacted by that day's unforgettable event.

ALVIN KOH'S TESTIMONY

I had an unusual dream before Dr. Joe Ozawa came to minister at our church in May 1992. In the first part of my dream, I was walking along the road and encountered many people trying to get my attention to help them. I refused and went on my way. In the second part, I was taken up to heaven and heard a voice asking me, "What have you done for the kingdom of heaven on earth?" I was unable to respond. In the morning I woke up with cold sweat on my forehead as I was deeply convicted by that dream. For the first time in my life, I realized that while Jesus was my Saviour, He was not my Lord. I repented and invited Him that very day to come and be the Lord of my life. I felt a deep sense of peace afterwards.

Two nights later, I had a second dream. This time I saw many young people falling down to the ground while they were receiving prayer in the front of our church. I had no idea what that dream was about but it really intrigued me.

That weekend, Dr. Joe Ozawa came and taught us about the Holy Spirit. He said during his message, "There are some people here who had dreams, and you already know what God will do today."

In my heart, I felt that he was speaking directly to me. I decided to sneak upstairs to the nursery that overlooked the sanctuary through a wide glass panel so I could have a better view of the meeting down below.

After his message, Dr. Ozawa invited the young people to come to the front for prayer. As they were being prayed for, I saw one by one falling down under the power of the Holy Spirit. It was exactly like in my second dream. I came from a Brethren background and had never seen anything like this in my life. Although I was very skeptical, the dream I had had actually prepared me for what we were experiencing at that time.

"Test the spirit" was what I heard next in my spirit. So I prayed, "Lord show me if this is you."

Instantly, I was so powerfully touched by the Holy Spirit that I was shaking and crying uncontrollably. For the first time, I truly felt the Father's love as I was filled with the Holy Spirit. I also felt a deep assurance of my salvation. Dr. Ozawa and his team prophesied that God would call me to the unity movement to see healing come to the body of Christ. I was overwhelmed with those words as they seemed so impossible at the time.

Then, we were asked to come to the front so Dr. Ozawa could brief us on what just happened. As I made my way along the aisle, I still remember clearly what I did: I went up to Perry and vigorously patted him on his shoulders with my right hand. At that time, it didn't mean much to me. Ten years later, Perry was the elder who stayed and walked closely with me as we persevered to rebuild the church through the next phase of its journey.

Many of us who were touched that weekend met together to pray and support each other through this experience. I was so hungry I would wake up at 3 a.m. to pray and read my Bible. The Word of God became alive in me. It wasn't just printed words. It became life-giving. At this time, God began to speak to me in powerful ways and I learned that He really wanted a close and intimate relationship with me.

Looking back, many of our leaders now realized that God in His mercy had come to give us a wake-up call in May 1992. In 2002, the Holy Spirit came upon the church again, but this time it was to awaken the next generation. Today, He has brought the two generations together so we could build His church His way rather than the ways of men. What a privilege it is to be part of God's amazing family!

JONATHAN KOH'S TESTIMONY

I remember Joe Ozawa's weekend visit to our church in 1992. And I remember him speaking from Acts 19:

"While Apollos was at Corinth, Paul took the road through the interior and arrived at Ephesus. There he found some disciples and asked them, "Did you receive the Holy Spirit when you believed?"

They answered, "No, we have not even heard that there is a Holy Spirit."

So Paul asked, "Then what baptism did you receive?"

"John's baptism," they replied.

Paul said, "John's baptism was a baptism of repentance. He told the people to believe in the one coming after him, that is, in Jesus."

On hearing this, they were baptized in the name of the Lord Jesus. When Paul placed his hands on them, the Holy Spirit came on them, and they spoke in tongues and prophesied." (Acts 19:1-6)

What he shared made me want to hear more.

I was born in Singapore to a Christian family. Baptized as an infant in the Anglican Church, I grew up attending Sunday school and was confirmed at age 13. I attended Youth Fellowship at my church and went to their annual youth retreats. You can say that I came from a typical bible-based, Evangelical church with a standard understanding of salvation by faith in Jesus.

When I heard Joe preach from Act 19:1-6, I found myself identifying with the disciples that Paul met in Ephesus who had received John's baptism of repentance. But I had no understanding or experience of the baptism of the Holy Spirit.

Joe Ozawa was an unusual speaker. Laid back in manner, he spoke in an easy conversational way and was not overly serious. He kept a gentle tone of voice when he preached and was neither loud nor dramatic. He did not try to stir up people's emotions in any way. He just spoke plainly and simply.

Towards the end of the service, he invited people forward for prayer. First he called the Elders, next, the Deacons, followed by the cell group leaders. As I was a cell group leader at that time I went to the front. I did not know what to expect because this was not a typical practice at my church.

While Joe prayed, my eyes were closed and my heart was directed to Jesus. As Joe prayed for gifts of prophecy and tongues to be released, I heard people suddenly start speaking in tongues. This surprised me as I had never seen that before. Then he prayed for people to receive the gift of singing in the spirit. I thought to myself that that would be kind of cool but I didn't feel anything. He also prayed for gifts of healing to be released. But I didn't feel anything either.

He then prayed for people to know God's love. Sounds of people crying could be heard. Through my half-opened eyes I saw people falling onto the floor. There were prayers for other gifts to be released as well. But, I still did not experience anything.

Meanwhile, as things were happening around me, I was trying to figure out what was going on. I had been attending church for the past four years, however, nothing like this had ever happened in our church service before.

Towards the end of the ministry session, Joe prayed for people that God would call to missions. Suddenly I felt God grip my heart. A sense of love so deep and overwhelming led me to just cry out. I felt myself being pressed slowly to the ground. God's empowering love for the people of the world and His longing for them to know Him washed over me.

The words of a song that I had learnt at a Youth Fellowship retreat in Singapore came to mind:

> *Strike in me a flame, Lord*
>   *this is my desire*
> *Life is not a game, Lord*
>   *set my soul on fire*
> *Give me eyes to see, Lord*
>   *help my heart to feel*
> *Do a work in me, Lord*
>   *Fashion something real*
>
> *Hate is all around, Lord*
>   *Where has man gone wrong?*
> *Can't a cure be found, Lord*
>   *Must we wait so long?*
> *Show me how to love, Lord*
>   *people everywhere*

> *Send it from above, Lord*
>   *all that I can share*
>
> *Move within my heart, Lord*
>   *Start this very hour*
> *Conquer every part, Lord*
>   *Work with mighty power*
> *You for every soul, Lord*
>   *Died upon a tree*
> *Let me share this goal, Lord*
>   *Setting people free*

In due course, God led me on short term mission trips to Guatemala (1992), Taiwan (1995), and South Africa (2002). Later, sensing the need for further equipping for mission work I did my theological training at Tyndale Seminary (1999-2001). This was followed by practical ministry training at Ellel (2002) and Singing Waters (2003).

From 2003 to 2006, I served as a missionary in South Africa. During that time, I lived in a black township with the Xhosa people, sharing life with them, learning their language and culture, and loving them with the love that God placed in my heart.

Looking back, I view that day in 1992 as a significant milestone in my Christian journey."

(Note: Jonathan Koh was a Deacon at the time. He is currently serving as an Elder in the church.)

As you can read from both Alvin's and Jonathan's testimonies, the Holy Spirit was clearly working in our midst to bring spiritual awakening and revival to the church. However, there was doubt and confusion in those days with many wondering if this was truly a visitation from God.

It might seem a coincidence but we were tested the following Sunday when we had another guest speaker who came from a local Baptist church. He spoke strongly from the pulpit, warning us against preachers who encouraged people to seek spiritual experiences that might lead to emotionalism and demonic deception. Some were wondering out loud:

"Is this the Lord's warning to us to steer clear of uncontrolled spiritual manifestations that disrupt the orderly form of worship in church?"

That message certainly had the most dampening effect over what we had just witnessed and experienced the previous weekend. A meeting was immediately called by the Pastor and church leaders to deal with the situation.

After much discussion, the consensus was that we should not rush to form any judgement but should let things settle down while we mulled over a recommended reading of a book by John White entitled, "When the Spirit comes with Power." In the book, the author dealt with topics of which the church had little knowledge or experience, such as uncontrollable shaking, sudden falls during prayer, unexpected weeping or laughter, dramatic healings, prophecy and visions, and encounters with demonic spirits. The question the author posed was, "Is it mass hypnosis, demonic deception, or genuine revival?"

In the absence of a clear voice, the church leadership decided to shut down what we now know was a move of the Holy Spirit to wake up the church for the first time at MSBC. Admittedly, it was safer to keep the status quo doing church the way we used to rather than to expose ourselves to what seemed rather unwieldy and unpredictable. As time went on, we became once again a normal, traditional church. And for the next seven years, Sunday service was as orderly and predictable as the Order of Worship printed in the weekly church bulletin.

In conversation with Dr. Ozawa who was invited to come again ten years later in 2002, we were totally surprised when he shared with us that what happened at MSBC in 1992 was the first time he himself had encountered such a powerful move of God within a church. Since then, he admitted that he had not seen a similar occurrence in all the churches he had been invited to speak and minister to in other parts of the world.

CHAPTER 9

A SECOND CHANCE

We have a natural resistance to change since it's difficult to foresee the benefit it may or may not bring. "Better to be safe than sorry" is what we will often say to ourselves as we retreat into our comfort zone. How can we have a breakthrough if we choose to remain in a cocoon when God's design, as the following Scripture says, is for us to be set free to soar like the eagle?

"Even youths grow tired and weary, and young men stumble and fall; but those who hope in the Lord will renew their strength. They will soar on wings like eagles; they will run and not grow weary, they will walk and not be faint." (Isaiah 40:30-31)

In 1999, there was a stirring among the young people when a guest speaker was invited by Victor Koh, our Associate Pastor, to speak at their Sunday service. Dr. Paul White had previously served as a pastor with a Vineyard church in Toronto. Besides preaching the good news, he was also passionate about setting people free through healing and deliverance in the power of the Holy Spirit. What happened then was a prelude to what the Holy Spirit would later do at another retreat of the young people held at Emily Lake in 2000. It would seem that the Spirit was working to change our young people whose lives, according to the confessions that emerged later on, were wrought by drugs, sin, and shame.

Joe Chong was present at both these retreats. This is his account of what he saw and experienced first-hand as a young adult. His life has since been turned right-side up after his personal encounter with the Holy Spirit.

JOE CHONG'S TESTIMONY

"At Emily Lake, I encountered the Father's Heart in a profound and life-changing way. It was at the end of one afternoon session. Following his message on Holiness, Adrian (our Youth Pastor) asked us to turn to a page in a booklet we had received in which was a list of various sins. We were to look at each sin and put a check-mark beside each one we were involved in. I went through the list and ended up checking every sin that I did or was involved in. After that, he told us to stand up and form a line if we would like to receive prayer. Everyone stood up and took his or her place in the line. Each of us had the booklet in hand and the list of all the sins that we had committed.

Adrian asked us to close our eyes and enter into a time of worship. I clearly remember the words of the song, 'Breathe' (sung by Michael W. Smith) being played over and over again:

> *This is the air I breathe.*
> *This is the air I breathe*
> *Your holy presence*
> *Living in me*

This is my daily bread
This is my daily bread
Your very word
Spoken to me
And I I'm desperate for you
And I I'm lost without you

Adrian then asked us to confess our sins to God and let the Holy Spirit minister to us.

I began to pray to God, confessing all of my sins. As I was asking Him for forgiveness, something profound happened to me. It was an experience that changed my life for good. Prior to Emily Lake, I had a hard time trying to hear the voice of God and learn what it meant to have an intimate relationship with Him. However, after confessing my sins, I began to hear the voice of God more clearly while standing in line with my eyes closed. I felt everything fading away. It was just God and me standing there. In spite of all my sins and ugliness, God was still saying to me that He loved me. It was at that moment that I truly understood and felt the Father's unconditional love for me. He was not looking at all my wrongdoings. All He saw was the good in me because He created me to be who I am to him, His beloved child. I was deeply touched by His heart and love for me.

After Emily Lake, I began to develop an intimate relationship with my Heavenly Father, earnestly seeking Him with the desire to know the secret things of His heart. I wanted to know this God who loved me so much and so unconditionally. I became more obedient to Him, more willing to follow His ways. The more I sought after Him, the more He revealed himself to me and the things of His heart. I started to notice His heart for the poor, the lost, and the broken. It was out of encountering the Father's Heart that I started to allow God to move in my life. The things of His heart became the things of my heart."

(Note: Joe Chong was a youth leader in those days who spent much time with the young people, walking with them as a big brother. Many have benefitted from his godly influence and care.)

CHAPTER 10

REVIVAL TENSIONS

When we look back over our journey, I'm sure we'll see some significant events that have redirected our course. Certain events seem to be designed to prepare us for what lies ahead, including rough patches and unexpected storms that may shake us up…individually, as a family or (in our case) corporately as a church. Here is my recollection of what actually happened following what we now see as the second move of God in our midst.

While it was good to see most of our young people fired up as a result of their encounter with the Holy Spirit at the Emily Lake retreat in 2000, it was disconcerting for the church leaders and parents to observe the sudden change in their behaviour in church. Some were giving prophetic words to one another while others were starting to speak in tongues in their weekly gatherings.

However, what was more disturbing to some parents was the openness of their sons or daughters in confessing, either at home to their parents or in church to the youth pastor, their drug or pornographic addictions.

I recall one evening joining the young people during their

weekly worship where I was prompted to release this word found in 2 Timothy 1: 6-8.

"For this reason I remind you to fan into flame the gift of God, which is in you through the laying on of my hands. For God did not give us a spirit of timidity, but a spirit of power, of love and self-discipline. So do not be ashamed to testify about our Lord."

Why give such a word to fire them up when it would have been more prudent to tone down? The truth was that, given what I observed that evening, I was so moved in my own spirit that I couldn't hold back the word. The young people were so passionate in worship, so earnest in seeking to dwell in God's presence, any observer would have been moved to urge them on.

Needless to say, there was much tension within the church body in those days. Many were openly questioning if the young people were being deceived by the influence of the youth pastor leading the group. Some were accusing Adrian Wi and Victor Koh for taking the young people to attend revival conferences held at The Airport Church (TACF) where it was well-known that manifestations often occur when people were touched by the Holy Spirit during ministry time.

Serving as an Elder in the church leadership, I felt constrained and opted not to take a position for the sake of keeping the peace whenever the leaders met to discuss the situation. Choosing to defer to the Senior Pastor, as most Deacons did, we decided not to rock the boat but to let things cool down without further action.

HEALING & DELIVERANCE

In May 2003, two seasoned gifted speakers—Dr. Paul White from Vineyard Church and Steve Chua from Singing Waters Ministries—were invited by Victor Koh (our Associate Pastor) to give our young people some training in Healing & Deliverance. It was held at Salvation Army's Jackson Point Camp with around 30 adults joining in.

Paul White was earlier invited to speak at our Sunday service. I still remember what he shared in his message because it struck a chord in me. As an elder in church whom people look up to for advice and prayer answers, I could relate with what he said about ministering repeatedly to hurting people. Here's a gist of what he shared:

"I've been a pastor for the past 20 years. From time to time, people in church would approach me to pray for them. Whether they're hurting from marital conflicts or struggling with broken relationships or other issues, I would counsel and pray for them. They seemed relieved when they leave but time and again, these same people would return seeking further help from me. Even though I already have a Master of Divinity degree, I thought I should go for further studies to be better equipped. So I took up a Ph.D. course in Counseling thinking I could be a more effective pastor to serve my congregation. However, even after my further studies, I saw the same pattern of behaviour in spite of my prayerful counsel for those who came to seek my help. And it was out of desperation that I turned to the Bible to read all the gospels over and over again. That's when my eyes were opened to see what Jesus did when he was among the people who were following him. He wasn't just preaching the kingdom of God; he was also healing the sick and driving demons out of people's lives. This brought a new direction in my ministry, causing me to seek training in healing and deliverance and practising it in my ministry till I was released by God years later to preach and minister in healing and deliverance in Brazil and in different parts of the world."

Both speakers spoke and taught passionately about the Holy Spirit and the work He was doing to heal and set people free from demonic oppression and bondages. They also encouraged both the adults and young people to be open to receiving all the spiritual gifts the Holy Spirit wanted to release—including the gift of prophecy and speaking in tongues—in order to equip believers to carry out Jesus' mission on earth. Many were inspired and touched as a result, especially the young people who were greatly stirred by the manifestations they experienced or saw in others during ministry time.

Moved by both speakers through their teaching with practical illustrations leading to the deliverance of a young adult (a friend brought by a member) who was spiritually oppressed, a group of four (Adrian, Audrey, Perry and Catherine) went on to attend the Isaiah 61 Summer School—a month of teaching and training in healing and deliverance held at Singing Waters in Orangeville.

We went even though there was a pandemic, called SARS, in those days that was infecting many in Toronto and elsewhere around the world. Because of SARS, we had a much smaller class of around 35, mostly adults, of various backgrounds from New York, New Jersey, Toronto, Yukon, and the U.K, as well as a family of three from Australia.

Looking back, I consider this to be another exciting new season for me. My eyes were opened to see the need for inner healing and deliverance from strongholds or bondages controlling our minds and emotions. Even when we started with worship on the first day, it was a startling experience for me to see some students spontaneously shaking or manifesting as we sang and prayed for the Holy Spirit to come in our midst.

Each teaching session served to give us an increasing understanding of the Creator God who created us in His image and who loves each person unconditionally.

"Therefore, brothers, we have an obligation—but it is not to the sinful nature, to live according to it. For if you live according to the sinful nature, you will die; but if by the Spirit you put to death the misdeeds of the body, you will live, because those who are led by the Spirit of God are sons of God. For you did not receive a spirit that makes you a slave again to fear, but you received the Spirit of sonship. And by Him we cry, 'Abba, Father.' The Spirit Himself testifies with our spirit that we are God's children." (Romans 8:12-16)

According to the Word of God, we are sons and daughters of a loving faithful Father. That's our identity in Christ! However, our identity could become distorted because of the sins in our lives or the deep hurts and pains caused by others which we still harbor within us. We all need to be set free by the renewing of our mind with the truth revealed in Scripture. We were taught to deal with six root causes that Satan could use to plant negative and resentful thoughts in our mind about ourselves or others: Culture, Generational Sins, Parents, Authority Figures, Intimate Relationships, and Life Experiences.

Every session in the class was eye-opening as we delved into each of these six roots. Following each session, it was very encouraging to hear the testimonies of those who were set free from brokenness and rejection when a root cause was identified, renounced, and cast out through prayer. This indeed was a life-changing experience for me and everyone who came to the school! Thank God we all came in spite of the prevalent threat of SARS that continued to spread in Toronto and in different parts of the world.

Taking a month off was a rare treat for both Catherine and I in view of the time-sensitive nature of our sales promotion business. Surprisingly there were no unexpected or urgent calls from our clients while we were at the school. It gave us the opportunity to absorb everything that was taught. More importantly, as a result of what we saw and experienced, we began to develop a passion for this ministry—a passion that led to many exciting encounters as we put into practice what we had learned. To teach, pray and minister to people who were open to inner healing both in and outside our church.

We were thinking of resuming our business after the month off work but apparently (as I shared in Chapter 6) this was not part of God's plan. We had to eventually shut down Dynacom Graphics Inc. which led to my retirement from secular work at the age of 60.

Meanwhile a storm was looming over the church that would shake it to its core. In hindsight, it was a timely blessing that Catherine and I were given the opportunity to first be healed and restored during the Isaiah 61 Summer School. Thank God that having been relieved of the work pressure in running a business, we had a sense of peace and calm even though church leadership meetings were heating up in those days. There was increasing disunity within the church and acrimony primarily directed against the young people and those who chose to support them. In spite of the ban imposed on the young people against attending TACF, many could not resist going to their spiritually-charged meetings and conferences. This added to increased tension and division among the adults.

CHAPTER 11

CHURCH SPLIT

We celebrated the 22nd Anniversary of the church in April 2003. However, the atmosphere at this point was riled with suspicion as the congregation was clearly divided into two camps: one favoring the familiar set order in worship with traditional hymns, and the other longing for the Holy Spirit's presence and touch in an extended time of free-flowing worship.

It is true what Jesus said in Mark's gospel, *"If a kingdom is divided against itself, that kingdom cannot stand. If a house is divided against itself, that house cannot stand."* (Mark 3:24-25)

Who could have imagined that we would be facing a church split down the road because of the view held by each side regarding the Holy Spirit? We had heard of other churches splitting up because of the same issue, so it wasn't a problem the church leaders were unaware of. Yet it presented itself as a problem over time. Would the young people and those who supported them back down so we could continue with the traditional way of worship and ministry? After all, it had taken the church 22 years to build and grow a 300-strong congregation in its weekly

Sunday attendance. Who in their right mind would want the church to split?

However, it was strange how things came to a head so unexpectedly. Some leaders knew we were at a crossroad but this only became apparent to others as the following events unfolded around June 2003. Having felt God's call to move to the West, Pastor Victor Koh tendered his resignation after accepting a pastoral appointment with a Chinese church in Vancouver. Around the same time, Pastor Adrian Wi was also planning to move West with his family; given his strong desire to minister to troubled youths, he was joining a mission organization called Urban Promise. Meanwhile, Senior Pastor John Tan also decided to tender his resignation in order to care for his wife, Gracie, who was suffering from cancer. Suddenly, we had three resignations on hand! And without collaborating with one another, all three pastors picked August 31, 2003 as their last day of work!

"There is a time for everything, and a season for every activity under heaven: a time to plant and a time to uproot…a time to tear down and a time to build…" (Ecclesiastes 3:3)

Were we facing a season of dramatic change that was beyond our control? Was this a time for the church to flow with the move of the Spirit rather than the traditions and opinions of men? The choice was clear for those who believe in the Holy Spirit. After all, this was what Jesus had promised His disciples before His crucifixion and ascension: *"If you love me, you will obey what I command. And I will ask the Father, and He will give you another Counselor to be with you forever—the Spirit of truth......But the Counselor, the Holy Spirit, whom the Father will send in my name, will teach you all things and will remind you of everything I have said to you."* (John 14:15-16; 26)

At a crossroad everyone has to decide which way to turn—right or left. This was the situation the church members faced as they wrestled with the thought of staying or leaving. Most of them had been with the church for many years and it was heart-breaking to leave the close relationships built over the years. Eventually, as more and more among the traditional group made the painful choice to leave, we were left with a remnant of less than a hundred people.

Thank God we had a remnant who chose to stay in spite of the fallout! Everyone was aware that the journey ahead would be tough but the church must stand firm and united in order to worship and serve God as a Body of Christ. As time went by, it was encouraging to see the commitment of the remaining members coming each Sunday in spite of the murmurings from some members who had left MSBC. These ex-members were apparently discouraging others from coming by saying the church had fallen under a spirit of deception.

However, with the change in atmosphere after the church split, we saw an increasing desire to seek the Lord and dwell in His presence—particularly among the young people. Worship was more spontaneous and free. In a paradigm shift that no longer constrained worshippers to hold back whenever moved by the Holy Spirit, we saw a greater measure of freedom and willingness to exercise spiritual gifts like speaking in tongues (provided there was interpretation), or the releasing of a prophetic word for the church (as long as it was done with proper pastoral supervision and in accord with God's Word).

"Therefore, my brothers, be eager to prophesy, and do not forbid speaking in tongues. But everything should be done in a fitting and orderly way." (1Corinthians 14:39-40)

A DIAMOND VISION FOR NEW SEASON

It would appear from our journey to this point that God knew what was going on and was preparing a chosen shepherd to lead the flock before and after the church split.

For it was earlier at the Salvation Army Jackson Point retreat in May 2003 that Alvin Koh was given permission by Pastor John Tan to share a vision he had received that he believed was from God for MSBC. Alvin presented it with a sketch, calling it a "Diamond Vision" because of its resemblance to a baseball diamond. This was before the church split.

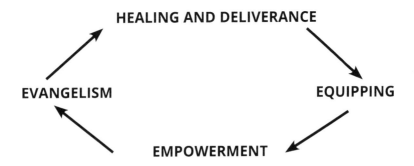

Secondly, although Pastor John Tan had decided to pass the mantle of leadership to Alvin Koh before he left, recognizing that God was giving us a new beginning, the church decided to seek the Lord's leading through prayer, fasting, and waiting upon him. The expectation was that changes could be made once the vision was cast and the church's purposes clarified so we could work together in love and unity; to find the answers that will set the church in a new direction. But at this point, being the only pastor remaining, Alvin himself wasn't sure he was qualified to lead the church.

What eventually convinced Alvin to accept his role as Lead Pastor came unexpectedly when he and his wife, Patricia, went on a trip to North Carolina with his parents and their two teenage children, Melanie and Darryl. Since this was a significant turning point not only for Alvin but the church as well, I felt it was important for Alvin to share in his own words this part of his journey.

LEAD PASTOR FOR LIFE-SPRING

"In May 2003, a group of around twenty members from our church went to Ottawa to attend a prophetic conference led by Graham Cooke. The prophetic ministry then was very new for most of us but we were keen to be taught to prophesy to one another. I partnered Hendrik Anthonio to receive a prophetic word from him. He drew a mountain and said that God would speak to me in a mountain. At that time, I thought his word was far-fetched. I was quite skeptical as there were no mountains in Ontario.

After the three pastors had announced their resignations, Perry asked me to pray about leading the church. To be frank, both Patricia and I felt like running away at that time! We felt totally inadequate. As well, all the problems associated with the move of the Holy Spirit in church made us very nervous and unsure.

When we returned from Ottawa, a friend offered her time-share unit for us to rest and seek God's heart and direction. Given her kind invitation, Patricia started looking for a suitable place to go. When she mentioned that she had found one that was available in Beech Mountain, North Carolina, I asked her to book it. Somehow, the mountain that Hendrik drew for me began to resonate in my heart.

We left Toronto very early in the morning and it was quite late when we approached Beech Mountain. As we were driving up Beech Mountain, we saw this huge 40-foot sign by the road…"River of Life Church. We are a different kind of church." I told my family, we need to go to this church on Sunday.

When we finally found this church on Sunday, there were only twelve members meeting in a small room in a hotel. I must say I was quite disappointed as I was expecting a big church with a big worship team matching the 40-foot sign. The service began with a lady reading John 1:46, *"Nazareth! Can anything good come from there?"* That immediately convicted me for I knew God was rebuking me for my wrongful thoughts. So I repented right away.

At the end of the service, the pastor asked if anyone needed prayer. Patricia and I immediately stepped forward as we wanted to know what God would have us to do at our church. We stood in a circle with the pastor and his prayer team. He first asked for permission to pray for Pat, and this was what he said, "You have been asking God what you are supposed to do....You are to be your husband's helpmate."

Wow! That immediately answered the question Pat had in mind.

Then he turned to me and said, "Are you seeking the Lord for direction?" As if I had the question written on my forehead, he asked, "Are you deciding on a senior position in a church?" He further said, "The Lord has prepared you for this role. He will help you carry it out."

Wow! Tears immediately flowed down to my cheeks. I was overwhelmed by God's goodness in answering so directly, through the pastor, the questions Pat and I had in our mind.

The next day, I woke up early before anyone else and decided to go to the mountaintop to read God's Word. It was a cold morning. I was shivering as I sat on a bench. So I moved back into the van to read. Following the "Read through the Bible Program," that day's reading was Ezekiel 34. This was what went through my mind as I read the following scriptures:

Verse 2: *"Woe to the shepherds of Israel who only take care of themselves! Should not shepherds take care of the flock?"* This sounded to me like a rebuke and not a call to lead.

Verse 11-12: *"I myself will search for my sheep and look after them. As a shepherd looks after his scattered flock when he is* with them, so I will look after my sheep." It's clear that Jesus will look after his sheep. Again this did not sound to me like a call.

Verse 23: *"I will place over them one shepherd, my servant, David, and he will tend them and will be their shepherd."* This clearly came across as the Lord's word for me for I was immediately filled with his Spirit and started to weep spontaneously. I could not imagine that God would pick me to lead his church.

Verse 26: *"I will bless them and the places surrounding my hill. I will send them showers in season; there will be showers of blessing."* This word further gave me the strength and courage to move forward.

As I returned to where we were staying, Pat asked me if God had spoken to me. I just gave her Ezekiel 34 to read without saying anything. After reading Ezekiel 34, Pat knew in her heart that God wanted us to accept the call to lead the church even though we felt thoroughly unqualified for the task ahead.

We drove to Beech Mountain not wanting the role. We encountered God in the River of Life Church as He spoke through the pastor to assure us of His help. God made it clear through Ezekiel 34 that we were to heed His word. Confusion and fear were replaced by His peace. This was what settled our minds to finally accept the call to lead the church."

So not only was Alvin given a "Diamond Vision" as God's blue-print for the church going forward, he was also given God's confirmation to take his place as the chosen shepherd to lead the flock in the new season.

Here's what I wrote in our official notice to the members of our 23rd Annual General Meeting held on April 3, 2004:

"As we reflect on the past year let us give thanks to God for His faithfulness in preserving His church in spite of the most painful and destabilizing period we have experienced in the history of MSBC.

He has been gracious to leave us a remnant who have chosen to stay and to see how the Holy Spirit will enable us to fulfill the "Diamond Vision" given to Pastor Alvin Koh as he takes up the mantle of pastoral leadership.

Now is the time for rebuilding our church, focusing on the things that are close to God's heart. Uniting the body of Christ through strong and transparent relationships. Encouraging one another toward love and good deeds. Fulfilling the mission of Jesus Christ to preach good news to the poor, heal the broken-hearted and set captives free. Enforcing our God-given authority and power in the name of Jesus Christ through prayer and intercession that the will of God may be done on earth as it is in heaven."

CHAPTER 12

ENCOUNTER WITH JESUS

In Spring 2004, I decided to attend a weekend stay-over course in Orangeville called SWAT ('Singing Waters Advanced Training') in order to receive further training in healing and deliverance. Jonathan Koh also attended, sharing a bedroom with me. This turned out to be the most significant event in my journey as a Christian given my encounter with Jesus during the time of personal ministry!

In the SWAT class, participants were assigned to groups of three to receive personal ministry in a private room led by a ministry staff. As instructed, we were to remain quiet and wait on the Holy Spirit after inviting Him to come. It was an amazing experience for me to observe from that point how spontaneously the ministry proceeded. When the person was moved in his spirit to openly share about the shame, hurts and pains caused by others—even during childhood—healing was evidently taking place when these hidden areas of darkness were exposed and forgiveness was released during the ministry session. Body shaking, tears and sobbing were the manifestations I saw in the two individuals—a young man serving in a well-known church in Toronto, and a 70-year old gentleman with his own accounting business—while they were being ministered to before me.

Given what I saw, I was somewhat nervous wondering what would surface from my past when my turn came. Would I shake and manifest like the other two? Even though I had received personal ministry during the Isaiah 61 School last year, I was interested to know if there were remaining areas in my life, past and present, that I needed to resolve to be set free of any unconfessed sins, bondages or darkness that could hinder my life as a follower of Christ.

Early in the morning, before my ministry time, I decided to take a walk along an unpaved road in the wooded outskirts of Singing Waters. The air was quite refreshing and sun rays were gleaming through the trees. Along the way, I came across a small running stream on the side. It caught my attention as I saw how clean and clear the water was. Fresh-looking ferns softly fluttering with the breeze lined both sides of the stream.

When my ministry time came, the group again sat in a circle after a brief prayer by the leading minister, Andy K. I kept my eyes closed as we waited quietly. After a few minutes, Andy asked if I sensed anything. I said "No". It was quite a long while with nothing happening when Andy patiently asked me again to tell him if I felt anything. Even though I had the urge to give up, Andy encouraged me to wait. So I kept waiting wondering when he was going to quit.

All of a sudden, an image appeared like a video in my mind. With my eyes still closed, I told the group what I saw:

"I see a small stream. I see clear water running down. Ferns softly moving on both sides."

Andy urged me to remain quiet and wait; to tell him if anything else was seen.

As we waited, another scene was emerging before me! This was what I actually saw and described in detail to the group:

"I see a figure in the distance. He is walking towards me. He has a staff in his hand. (I knew he was Jesus because I could see his white robe and a staff in his hand.) Jesus is standing in front of me now. I'm down on my knees. He is handing me the staff with both hands above me. I am reaching up with both hands to take the staff. He said "Feed my sheep."

At this point, I broke down and wept uncontrollably. Then I saw Jesus turned around and walked away, gradually disappearing toward where He came from earlier. After Andy prayed over me at the end of the ministry, we adjourned for lunch in the dining room.

I must admit that during lunch time I was questioning in my mind whether I had actually seen Jesus or was it my imagination. Since there was a walking trail running through the woods at Singing Waters, I decided to go for a stroll by myself. Along the way, I picked up a fallen branch, stripped it down to a pole so I could protect myself in case I come across any wild animal in the woods.

It was a pleasant walk along the wide but shallow stream running through the woods. I could hear the soft gurgling sound of the flowing water. (I later found out it was this sound from which Singing Waters derived its name as given by Kay Golbeck, its founder.) Going upstream along the way, I came to a narrow sunken strip of land with a tiny brook running below. As I jumped across the water, I noticed something on the ground. Picking it up, I was surprised to see its features and shape; clearly resembling a shepherd's staff, just like what I had seen during my ministry time! (see photo)

Rejoicing with praise and excitement as I continued my walk back to the retreat center, I thanked God for this "mountain-top" experience. It somewhat reminded me of Moses and the staff God gave him before he was asked to lead the Israelites out of Egypt. How gracious Jesus was towards me in handing me the staff! He knew that given my practical and analytical mind, it would be hard for me to simply believe and accept what I saw and what He said to me in the vision. The staff was His confirmation, a tangible evidence I could hang on to, and to treasure in my heart as long as I live.

In the afternoon, each participant in the school was asked to share a testimony. Before this took place, I hid the staff behind some chairs on the podium. When my turn came, I started by asking:

"Can anyone tell me, what's this I am picking up behind me?"

Seeing the staff now held upright by my side, several voices responded, "A shepherd's staff". With that as an introduction, I then proceeded to share the vision I had received during my ministry time. It was good to have Andy standing by, nodding with tacit support as my witness.

For as long as I live I will never forget my encounter with Jesus. Even so, I chose to keep this within myself because I felt the vision was a personal revelation from God…not to be shared with others unless I was asked. As an Elder in the church, I could see why Jesus would ask me to feed His sheep given my responsibility to teach and preach the Word of God. So the vision remained a well-kept secret for many years until I was released to share it after attending a Prophetic Conference at TACF.

CALL TO BE A PASTOR

What happened at this crowded conference? First, it was Andy K. who happened to walk by where I was seated. Both of us were surprised to see each other. "Hey, Pastor Perry!" he called out. He mentioned in conversation that he still remembered the shepherd staff I picked up at Singing Waters. Secondly, as the conference was proceeding with increasing intensity in praise and worship, a young lady rushed onto the stage with a staff in her hand and excitedly proclaimed that she had received a word from the Lord. And the word was for those who already have a staff in their possession:

"The Lord wants you to rise up and take your place as His shepherd for His flocks!" she declared.

I must say that this was the first time I had received such a strong prompting to be a pastor. I had not been interested in such a position and had been turning down Pastor Alvin's offer, year after year, whenever he asked me if I would consider accepting a pastoral appointment in church.

FIRST MISSION TRIP

But the call to be a pastor was confirmed when we went on an unplanned trip to a native reserve in Lumberton, North Carolina. This was what happened.

Leonard John, a native evangelist, was invited to conduct a 5-day revival meeting in a native church, and he had asked Adrian and Sherene to join him in Lumberton. When Catherine and I found out that no one from the church was going with the couple, we volunteered to go. This was our first mission trip. We thought we could help take care of their two young children whom they were bringing along while they minister with Leonard John during the meeting. Along the way, Adrian wisely suggested that I should not call myself an Elder since natives tend to revere elders in their culture and they might keep their distance from me.

"Call yourself a pastor," he said.

Thus I went willingly accepting the pastor's title without expecting any need for me to act as one.

However, from time to time during the meeting, I was asked by the worship leader to go up the stage.

"Pastor Perry, would you pray for us before we start our worship?"

"Pastor Perry, please pray for those who need the Lord's healing tonight."

By joining Leonard and Adrian to pray and minister, I had the privilege to witness how spontaneously people, touched by the Holy Spirit, would break out in tongue or laughter whenever someone was healed of a sickness or pain in the body. You could sense the tangible presence of God as they raised their voices to praise and worship Him!

One night towards the end of a meeting, I happened to see a teenager sitting all alone at the back with his head bowed down. Even though I felt tired and wanted to leave with our team, I went across the aisle and tried to talk to him. He kept silent with his head looking down. I had to go on my knees in order to look at his face.

He told me his name was Lucas.

I said, "Lucas, Jesus loves you. Would you like to ask him to come into your life as your Savior tonight?"

He nodded his head. And face-to-face, I led him in a prayer to receive Jesus Christ as his Savior and Lord. What a joy it was for me to sense the Lord's love and compassion for Lucas that night, granting him the greatest gift he could ever receive—the gift of salvation through Jesus Christ!

The next evening before worship started, I had a bigger surprise. The worship leader at the front excitedly announced that her son, Lucas, had received Jesus into his life. The mother had apparently seen the change in her son at home and wanted the church to rejoice with her family. As we were adjourning to the kitchen for supper at the close of the meeting, I met Lucas standing at the corridor and was taken aback to see the change in his countenance. No longer looking downcast and shy, he smiled as I talked with him.

What I experienced in this mission trip marked another turning point in my journey. I felt my heart was opening more to the call of God to serve His church as a pastor. And at 65, when it would be customary for most people to retire from regular employment, Pastor Alvin asked me again if I was interested in joining the church staff as a House Pastor. This time, I readily said: "Yes."

ALASKAN MISSION TRIP

One event led to another and what followed was another mission trip in May 2009, led by Adrian & Sherene to Alaska. Leonard John had arranged with several native churches for us to do a Worship Conference in Anchorage and Fairbanks; 21 adults and 3 kids went on this trip.

By this time, many of our young people and adults had been trained and equipped, not only to preach but also to minister in inner healing (given the training they received from the Healing & Deliverance courses they had taken in church). There, teams were organized and allotted to speak and minister in different churches and locations over a period of two weeks.

In Mark's Gospel, we read the following Scripture at the end, *"Then the disciples went out and preached everywhere, and the Lord worked with them and confirmed his word by the signs that accompanied it."* (Mark 16:20) This was what I personally experienced on the first morning of the Worship Conference held in a large church in Fairbanks, Alaska. The first morning, as our worship team began to practise on-stage at the front, I went to the back of the sanctuary with the intention to welcome and usher any visitor in. Facing the stage, I felt a tap on my shoulder shortly after. The man behind said to me:

"I was released from prison this morning. As I walk past the church entrance just now, God told me I have been robbing him."

After emptying his pocket, he said: "I don't have much money with me. This is all I have. Can you give this to the person who is preaching Jesus in this place?"

This man, an ex-prisoner, was handing me all the money he had even though he needed it much more than us! I tried to turn him down but knew in my heart that he was probably convicted by the scripture in which God said: *"Will a man rob God? Yet you rob me…in tithes and offerings."* (Malachi 3:8)

Since he was adamantly asking me to accept the money, I told him that I would hand it over to Leonard John, the native evangelist. He then turned around and left the building before I could pray for him. When we counted the money, mainly loose change and a few US dollar notes, this was what he brought: seventeen dollars and twenty-two cents. What an incredible sign it was to see how God was working in our midst…even before the Worship Conference started!

By his act of repentance, I believe this man (probably an American) was redeemed by the grace of God on that day. Praise the Lord for confirming His words through this unforgettable experience in this second mission trip of mine.

Given the privilege to represent the church, this time as a bona fide pastor, I was able to connect with most of the native leaders, including the Mayor of a small community in Minto. I also led a team which gave us the opportunity to see how the Holy Spirit was working through us to impart God's love, comfort, and healing wherever we were sent. Being called a pastor did help in my interaction with others. Whereas the title did make me sense a difference within me, it was the Holy Spirit's presence that brought the greatest joy, enabling our team to speak and minister with His power to touch and restore many of the natives who came.

CHAPTER 13

BREAKTHROUGH WITH A NEW NAME

Looking back to the early days in 2004, I believe that God's hand was actively guiding Pastor Alvin Koh and the leadership team in navigating our way to rebuild the church with a smaller congregation. This was one of the Scriptures that we often quoted and hung on to after the church split:

"Forget the former things; do not dwell on the past. See, I am doing a new thing! Now it springs up; do you not perceive it? I am making a way in the desert and streams in the wasteland." (Isaiah 43:18-19)

We were now more sensitive to the Holy Spirit's leading and more willing to embrace the new things that He began to put in our path. Even changing the name of the church, a thought that we had resisted for the past 23 years!

This momentous move started April 17, 2004 with a proposal to review the church name in view of the increasing number of newcomers in the congregation who were neither Malaysians nor Singaporeans. The leadership team was quite open and united at this stage. Everyone agreed to pray and wait upon the Lord for a new name, however long this might take.

At a later leadership meeting, Pastor Alvin Koh shared what God had impressed upon his heart concerning His direction for the church for the next three years based on another Scripture from the Book of Isaiah:

"This year you will eat what grows by itself, and the second year what springs from that. But in the third year sow and reap, plant vineyards and eat their fruit." (Isaiah 37:30)

Could this be another prophetic word from the Lord to encourage us to look forward to growth and fruitfulness in the next three years?

What followed was another period of praying and waiting on the part of the intercessors. Finally, after six months of waiting, we had a consensus to change the name to "TORONTO LIFE-SPRING CHRISTIAN FELLOWSHIP" (hereinafter referred as 'Life-Spring'). An announcement was then made to the congregation, on a Sunday in December, just two days before Christmas!

Having a new name was an auspicious start for the New Year (2005). For it allowed the church to welcome all attendees regardless of their nationality, and to flow with the move of the Holy Spirit, following the "Diamond Vision" that was adopted as the blue-print for God's growth plan for the church.

Here's the updated version currently shown in Life-Spring's website:

As shown below, a new logo was also created to mark our transition into the new season with the name change.

FLOWING OUT AS A LIFE SPRING

It would appear that a major breakthrough came only after the new name was officially endorsed by all members of the church. During our church retreat held at Redeemer University College in 2005, a prophecy was released by our guest speaker, Dennis Ignatius, the Malaysian Ambassador at that time.

Apparently moved by the Holy Spirit, these were the words he declared over the church in his morning message:

> "You are going to walk in a liberty that you have not seen before, individually and corporately. You are going to walk in a new anointing and a new liberty that you have not seen before. And I praise God for that. He has been preparing a people for Himself. He is bringing you to that place."

As soon as he said this, we all heard a loud thunder BOOM; it shook the auditorium!

This unusual event marked a new phase of our journey—a season of growth and acceleration—as we progressively moved in step with the "Diamond Vision". Recognizing the need to be trained and equipped, we had already taken the first step in September 2001 by signing up with Evangelism Explosion (EE), an institution that taught and coached believers to share the Gospel with their friends and people in their social circle. By 2003, we had 19 EE trainees graduating from the 13-week course. We then took the bold step in partnering with Willowdale Pentecostal Church to host an EE Leadership Clinic for 28 pastors/church leaders from Ontario and Quebec. As a result, many of our members were able to reach out and pray for people outside the church and a number of converts started coming to Life-Spring.

HEALING & DELIVERANCE MINISTRY

In 2005, we started a bi-weekly class to teach inner healing and deliverance. The timing was right as we already had ten members who had gone through some healing and deliverance (H&D) courses conducted by Singing Waters; we had raised a team who could teach and minister in the class.

Initially open to church members, we knew from the testimonies we received that many were healed and restored from past hurts and pains. Bondages and strongholds were broken by the power of the Holy Spirit as they were set free during ministry time. As word got out, mainly from those who were healed, we were thrilled to see more and more outsiders from other churches coming to the class, including some pastors who came with some of their members. Beginning with a Part I introductory course lasting seven sessions, we later extended this life-changing ministry by offering a Part II course to go deeper in dealing with the six root causes that affect our outlook and identity. Eventually, given the interest of those who completed Part I and II, we even introduced a Part III course—"Restoring the Foundations"—teaching such topics as Anger, Emotional Pain, Fears, Shame and Rejection. At this stage, participants from other churches were also encouraged to serve as volunteers in our H&D teaching/ministry team so they would be equipped to serve in this vital ministry in their own church.

I must say, this was the most exciting phase of my journey serving as a pastor at Life-Spring. Thank God, I was given the privilege to start this ministry with Anita Wong, who came just in time to serve the church as a part-time Pastor, after completing her course with Ellel, an international healing & deliverance ministry, while she was in Australia and England.

Given the life-transforming results I have seen in people's lives, I am increasingly passionate about the H&D ministry. I have even been motivated to pray and minister to strangers whenever prompted by the Holy Spirit to do so, once ministering to an American tourist travelling with us in our tour group while we were vacationing in Turkey.

CHAPTER 14

EMPOWERED FOR OUTREACH

Celebrating our 25th Church Anniversary in April 2006, we decided to extend our invitation to all the ex-members who had left after the church split. We were glad many of them came to enjoy with us the 10-course celebration dinner held in a spacious Chinese restaurant. Among the guest speakers whom we specially invited, recognizing their contribution and walk with us through difficult times, was Dennis Ignatius (author of "Fire Begets Fire") who had earlier released a prophetic declaration over Life-Spring at our church retreat in 2005. The other guest speakers were Dr. Siang-Yang Tan, our first pastor, and Donna Parachin and Steve Chua from Singing Waters.

Dennis Ignatius was invited to speak at our worship service the following Sunday. Once again, full of passion with a message God had impressed upon him to speak from 1 Kings 18, he urged the church to "press in, press in." He said there was so much more God wanted to do in us through the Holy Spirit. Dennis then declared that the fire of God would come upon the church and "fire teams" would be sent out into the surrounding neighborhood and other churches, and that we would be "fire carriers" to bring revival and new faith with the call to impact nations.

24-HOUR WORSHIP

What followed was a season of Spirit-led activities beginning with a monthly 24-hour Worship that Life-Spring started in 2006. This brought together a group of like-minded pastors who also felt the need to pray for God to move in the city and in their congregations. Participating churches would take turns to lead worship in 2-hour slots, starting on Friday at 7.00 p.m. and ending on Saturday at 7.00 p.m. Held in a different venue every third Friday depending on the location of the host church, it was very encouraging to see worshippers coming together month after month to intercede for the city and to pray for one another; earnestly seeking to stay in the Father's presence while praying through continuous worship and intercession.

If you check our website www.life-spring.org, you'll see the following statement regarding the mission of our church:

"Our mission is to glorify God by sharing the Good News with people through **EVANGELISM,** bringing them into the knowledge and reality of wholeness in Christ through **HEALING AND DELIVERANCE,** discipling them through **EQUIPPING,** and then releasing them to minister with **EMPOWERMENT** by the Holy Spirit… everything under-girded by **INTERCESSION.**

We adopted **"everything under-girded by intercession"** as our stance when the church was renamed "Toronto Life-

Spring Christian Fellowship". We chose to be guided as a Body of Christ by the Holy Spirit through prayer. Looking back, we were on the right track in our preparation to flow out as a life spring when we started the 24-hour Worship.

It was through the 24-hour Worship that an outreach group was formed to go downtown each month to feed the homeless at the Seaton House Shelter. This involved many hands, both the youths and adults, helping to prepare and hand out the sandwiches. It also opened an avenue for them to share their faith in Jesus and to intercede for those who were open to seeking God's help through prayer. From time to time, volunteers from other churches would also join us in this monthly outreach.

FEEDING HOMELESS & STREET PEOPLE

We also partnered with a ministry called Bread of Life to feed the homeless and street people downtown. Every Monday evening, a small group from the church would pick up pizzas and snacks donated by local businesses and hand them out in a street location where these people would gather week after week. Thanks to these committed volunteers, many mouths were fed for a period of over 10 years.

Another outreach door was opened when we were approached by the minister of the International Christian Center (ICC) to participate in feeding the street people outside her church on Friday evenings. ICC was known in the neighborhood for its ministry to the poor and needy. It was heart-warming to see how eager and engaged our life groups were, taking turns to prepare and cook the food (usually hot dogs and salads). This was a practical way for Life-Spring to serve and to share God's love with those who came, and to pray for those who needed a word of hope and encouragement.

"FIRE TEAMS"

God works in mysterious ways. As He declared through his prophet Isaiah *"For my thoughts are not your thoughts, neither are your ways my ways. As the heavens are higher than the earth, so are my ways higher than your ways and my thoughts than your thoughts."* (Isaiah 55:8-9)

In 2007, after serving with three ministries in the West over a period of 4 years—Urban Promise in Vancouver, Fraser Valley Christian Center in Abbotsford, Vancouver Native Pentecostal Church—Adrian Wi was redirected to return to Life-Spring with his family. Appointed as an Associate Pastor, he was assigned to lead the young people and to teach and prepare them to go into missions.

Given his passion to minister to people who need to experience the life-changing love of God and be restored through the power of the Holy Spirit, Adrian was just the right person to spearhead our next breakthrough into missions. God was evidently preparing him for this role, sending him out West for a season to work among the poor and hurting and with the indigenous people.

Here is Adrian's testimony which I have asked him to share as part of Life-Spring's story.

"All authority in heaven and on earth has been given to me. Therefore, go and make disciples of all nations, baptizing them in the name of the Father and of the Son and of the Holy Spirit, and teaching them to obey everything I have commanded you. And surely I am with you always, to the very end of the age." (Matthew 28:18-19)

These famous words of Jesus have echoed and mobilized thousands of believers for over two thousand years since his Resurrection. But a common mistake Christians have made is to associate the word 'nations' with geographical boundaries when it more accurately denotes tribes and people groups.

This was the insight revealed and instilled in me when I was attached to the Vancouver Native Pentecostal Church. Our Father's heart is not just for a local church, or a country, but for the nations, i.e. all people, including the indigenous people, the homeless, the poor and needy. It was with this revelation that I returned to Toronto Life-Spring Christian Fellowship in 2007, rejoining my church family whose love and support launched me into full-time ministry, and into missions both locally and abroad.

It seemed my return was in God's timing to activate the young people for missions. In my role as the Missions Pastor, it was a privilege to observe how most of our young people as well as many adults were moved by the Holy Spirit to capture the Father's heart for the nations. What ignited them was a radical passion to follow what God had inspired them to be and to do.

Whether it was participating at gatherings to reach students in graduate schools, serving meals to the homeless in the inner-city streets of Toronto, teaching and ministering to native tribes on mission trips to Northern Ontario, British Columbia, Alaska and Lumberton (North Carolina), as well as conducting workshops and conferences in Uganda, the message we shared remained the same:

1. God, our Father, loves all people, and

2. Through Jesus Christ, the Kingdom of God has come to save all people from the curse of sin and death.

When our people, together with those they reached, witnessed the supernatural realities manifested through the power of the Holy Spirit, everyone was in awe. This brought forth a singularity of heart where they were able to enjoy the favor of God and love for each other every time they go in a group to minister outside the church.

In 2009, through a church member's contact with a native grandmother in Kenora, we were approached to pray and contend for the life of a 5-year-old native boy at the Toronto Sick Kids Hospital. When we first saw him, lying in a coma state, attached to a ventilator and heart monitor, many were taken aback by his critical condition even though we were moved by the grandmother's faith in God to save him (see photo).

Taking turns to visit the hospital daily, we started and maintained a prayer vigil for the boy. This went on week after week with some of the family's native relatives and friends joining to pray for his recovery in the hospital. Eventually,

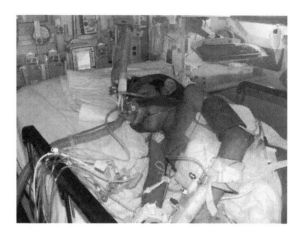

much to the joy of everyone involved, the boy regained consciousness and completely recovered. Thereafter, he was able to return to his home in Kenora, Ontario. Praise God for this unique opportunity to intercede with the family and witness this miraculous healing first-hand!

As a result, over 20 adults (from the older generation) were inspired to go on a mission trip to Kenora the following year. Working with a local pastor serving the First Nations, they ran a Vacation Bible School class, fed the poor and needy, preached and healed the sick in his church.

In my view, the mission for the church is clear. *"Go and make disciples of all nations, baptizing them in the name of the Father and of the Son and of the Holy Spirit, and teaching them to obey everything that Jesus commanded!"*

As Adrian has testified, indeed there were "fire teams" that went out to speak to youth groups in other churches and to student groups in different universities. Given the experience of seeing how powerfully the Holy Spirit was working in their midst, more and more of our young people were inspired to go whenever an invitation came. This turned out to be a much-needed preparation for greater things to come—mission trips to British Columbia, Alaska and Uganda!

In 2014, after leading many of our young people on short-term mission trips to Uganda starting in 2006, Adrian Wi was so moved by the brokenness of the people there (particularly a 19-month child in the orphanage), he took the bold step to move to Kampala, Uganda with Sherene and their three young boys. Working with the core leaders in churches to teach and train them to break the negative mindset of their people through healing in families and personal restoration, many have caught the vision to love and care for one another and to be equipped in order to be self-sufficient.

Amecet Ministries was founded by Adrian in 2019 in order to support the work being carried out through his ministry in Uganda as well as in Taiwan, Malaysia, Greece, Aboriginal and Inuit communities of Canada. It is registered as a Canadian charity and you can read its work as a mission organization at its website *www.amecet.com*.

MISSION IS THE OUTFLOW OF OUR VISION

Going on a mission trip with our church group can be an exciting, eye-opening experience when you first witness the manifestations of God through the Holy Spirit upon the people, especially those whose lives have been stricken with inner hurts, sickness or brokenness. This was our observation in most mission trips whether it be reaching indigenous groups living in poor native reserves in Canada or to poverty-stricken tribes housed in war-torn settlements in Uganda. It's truly a privilege to go in Jesus' name to touch a group of people with the love and comfort of God. And to work in step with the Holy Spirit to bring them hope, peace and renewal.

In the Gospel of John, Jesus said to his twelve disciples, *"I tell you the truth, anyone who has faith in me will do what I have been doing. He will do even greater things than these, because I am going to the Father."* (John 14:12)

We know from the gospel accounts that Jesus had instructed these disciples to follow his footsteps to preach the good news regarding the kingdom of God, to heal the sick and to drive out demons by the authority and power of his name. This, I believe, is what we are also called to do as followers of Christ! Praise God for the privilege of serving as bearers of His love and glory whenever He sends us out to minister to a people group or community.

EQUIPPING FOR GREATER WORKS

It would seem at this stage that we needed to be equipped for greater works of service according to God's Word: *"It was He who gave some to be apostles, some to be prophets, some to be evangelists, and some to be pastors and teachers, to prepare God's people for works of service, so that the body of Christ may be built up until we all reach unity in the faith and in the knowledge of the Son of God and become mature, attaining to the whole measure of the fullness of Christ."* (Ephesians 4:11-13)

So given our breakthrough experience with Dennis Ignatius at the church retreat in 2005, we would pray each year for a guest speaker to come and teach us during our Family Weekend (or annual retreat) held at Redeemer University College in Ancaster, Ontario. God was faithful in answering our prayer, looking at all the gifted ministers that He sent along to equip us as shown in the faith-building blocks below:

2018 Donna Parachin/Adrian Wi **LOVING THE JOURNEY**		2019 Wanda Fost **PRAYER & INTERCESSION**	
2015 Jerry Berengeur **BUILDING KINGDOM**	2016 35th Anniversary **CELEBRATION**		2017 Don Boyd **INTIMACY WITH GOD**
2013 Brian Sauder **RELATIONAL KINGDOM OF GOD**		2014 Donna Parachin **TOGETHER (FAMILY RELATIONSHIP)**	
2010 Clive Pick **OPEN HEAVEN**	2011 John Kelly **END TIME WARRIORS**		2012 Trisha Frost **THE HEART OF SONSHIP**
2008 Leonard John **UNITY OF THE SPIRIT**		2009 Michael Puffett **KEYS OF THE KINGDOM**	
2005 Dennis Ignatius **FIRE BEGETS FIRE**	2006 Jean Lim **KINGDOM POWER**		2007 Kirk Bennett **PRAYER & PROPHECY**

Apostles, Prophets, Evangelists, Pastor and Teachers, these were the speakers with the five-fold gifts who came to teach, minister and stretch us as part of our equipping.

PROPHETIC MINISTRY

In hindsight, the Lord has clearly been working to move us from one frontier to the next, sending to Life-Spring gifted preachers and speakers to give a timely word to prepare us for what God wanted to do in each season of our journey.

Even though the gift of prophecy is clearly identified as a gift we should "earnestly" and "especially" desire, it wasn't until we had experienced its power to reveal God's heart for the church that we began to accept and embrace the prophetic gift as part of our ministry. Listen to what the Scripture says: *"Follow the way of love and eagerly desire spiritual gifts, especially the gift of prophecy."* (1 Corinthians 14:1)

A good example is seen when Rev. Chua Wee Hian came, not only to teach but to guide us in the proper use of the prophetic gift in line with God's Word. Here's the prophecy he released over the church when speaking at our Sunday Service on July 8, 2007…a prophecy that proved to be true in propelling Life-Spring into frontiers of ministry we've not crossed before; a prophecy that shows that God does speak to those who are open to hearing His voice.

"God is saying this is a new season. New wine is flowing and new wine needs new wineskin. God is saying I am making all things new. Forget the past. Give thanks for the past but I'm doing new things you've never, never known before. I do not live on stale things or predictable things. I'm the God of the new, of things that are fresh and vibrant.

Life-Spring, your name is from me, says the Lord. The Lord says that you are going to bubble with life. You are going to be like streams flowing through the streets, ravines, valleys and so on, of Toronto and God is going to bring life through you. A few years ago, I preached to you about the river of life, that is true and Ezekiel tells us wherever the river flows there is life and you are called Life-Spring. You're going to bring the life and fullness of God to countless people here in this city and beyond.

The word from Scripture for you is from Isaiah 54—marvelous words. I want you to study them, read them—we have these prophetic words: *"Enlarge the place of your tent, stretch your tent curtains wide, do not hold back, lengthen your cords, strengthen your stakes for you will spread out to the right, and to the left. Your descendants will dispossess nations and settle in a desolate city."* Then later towards the end of this chapter, God says *"No weapon forged against you will prevail. And you will refute every tongue that accuses you. This is the heritage of the servants of the Lord."*

And then this prophecy is not only for this generation. It goes on to other generations because God is also saying all your sons and daughters will be taught by the Lord and great will be your children's peace or shalom. God is going to bless you not only this generation but the generation to come. So that to enlarge your tent, to strengthen the cords of relationship and God is going to multiply you and use you mightily.

And God is saying to Life-Spring members and leaders, from now on, you're not to be spectators. You're to be soldiers. Everybody hands on, hands on the job and God is going to use you mightily. And Life-Spring, one of the things God is also saying, "I'm raising up an army, a mighty army of spiritual warriors." And the strange thing is that you're not going to move as a big, cumbersome army, but you're going to move especially in platoons, smaller units, movable, adaptable units. And I believe this could refer to your cells, your small groups because your small groups are the ones that are going to be new churches, to plant new churches.

In our church in London, we planted a new church in the northwest; 5 or 6 cells were the ones that came together to form this new congregation. I believe God will do something like that through your church.

The other thing that God is saying is this: It's the time now for you to get your core values, your DNA, to write these down, because the churches you plant must have the DNA—when people come to Life-Spring and to your plants, they must see certain things that will say, "Yes, this is a Life-Spring church." This is the place where God is pleased to seal and to bless. Now you might hold your breath leaders, okay, hold your breath and gasp if you want to because God is going to provide you in the new future with a building, a building of your own in a very strategic place in Toronto. And He will provide things miraculously. You will be able to buy this building and use it as a training base to train leaders and to send them out.

Another thing that God is impressing on my spirit is that you will be a sending church. One of the things that God is going to use you greatly is to change your theology about the church. Many people think of church as a Sunday gathering, a Sunday assembly. It is the church.

But theologians rightly call it the church gathered, the church gathered. But God says the bigger church, the more effective church is not the church gathered, but the church scattered. And God is going to use you to bring healing, to release prophecy not only in a lovely building like this, a sanctuary like this but in a shopping mall, in the colleges, in the offices, on the streets and neighbourhood, even in leisure centers. God is going to do that. You're going to be a church scattered because you're going to bring in people.

So God is saying that to you and God will use you to build lots of churches throughout Toronto and beyond.

And finally, God is also saying something that—at the workshops, the leadership of the whole church must not think of things like what—if God wants it to happen it will happen. Nor are you to rely on pious wishes. I wish that this would take place and maybe have 10%, 20% bonus. That's not the thinking that God wants. The thinking that God wants to infuse and impart to this church is intentional. It must be purposeful, it must be prayed through. Plan carefully that these things will come to pass. So be intentional when you make your decisions. Don't just pray, don't just say "I wish this would take place." But God is going to use you greatly. And this calls for sacrifice, for discipline, for cohesion, for unity, and God the Holy Spirit will bring this about in this new season. Amen."

Note: Rev. Chua was the Senior Pastor of Emmanuel Evangelical Church in Westminster, London, UK. A seasoned preacher and teacher, he is well-regarded as a friend and mentor at Life-Spring

Years later, with increasing exposure to prophetic-gifted speakers like Graham Cooke, Ed Silvoso, Bill Johnson, Patricia King and Mike Bickle, a Prophetic Ministry was started at Life-Spring and still continues to the present time. Here's what I wrote in my report to the church to encourage everyone to get on board:

"We started our Prophetic Ministry on November 21, 2010 prompted by what the Word of God says in 1 Corinthians 14: *"Follow the way of love and eagerly desire spiritual gifts, especially the gift of prophecy… But everyone who prophesies speaks to men for their strengthening, encouragement and comfort… Therefore, my brothers, be eager to prophesy, and do not forbid speaking in tongues… But everything should be done in a fitting and orderly way."*

Our record shows that we conducted 126 sessions in total, prophesying over 116 individuals and 10 couples. Of the 126 receivers, 40 came from other churches while 27 were repeat receivers.

From the feedbacks received, it appears that the people who came have indeed been strengthened, encouraged and comforted. That's why some have come again and again, expecting a fresh word that would enable them to hear what the Lord is saying to help them to press on in their journey of life. While some have felt lifted in their spirit after the ministry, others have been moved by new insights of how God sees them—their true identity in Christ.

Have you ever asked the question why we have a Prophetic Ministry at *Life-Spring*? Apart from the fact that many have been touched by the affirming words received during ministry time, are there other reasons we should look at to understand why we need to have such a ministry in our church?

In the Gospel of John, Jesus clearly said *"I am the good shepherd"* and we are his sheep. *"He calls his own sheep by name and leads them out (of the sheep pen). When he has brought out all his own, he goes on ahead of them, and his sheep follow him because they know his voice. But they will never follow a stranger; in fact they will run away from him because they do not recognize a stranger's voice."* (John 10:3-5) Isn't it clear that we're expected to know Jesus as our shepherd by recognizing His voice when He calls us out by name?

Reason #1—Awareness: Learning to hear the voice of God is therefore the first reason why we need to have a Prophetic Ministry in place that will encourage people to be open to the truth that it's God's desire to speak to us, as a father would speak to his children out of his love and concern for their welfare. As Jesus was open to hearing from the Father at all times, so should we be open to hearing from Him. This is an **AWARENESS ISSUE**; the more you're aware of this, the more you'll want to hear His voice on a regular basis.

We all know that all spiritual gifts are given by the Holy Spirit for the common good of the body of Christ, enabling each person to serve others using whatever gift he/she has been given and received. Why did Paul single out the gift of prophecy as a spiritual gift we should eagerly and "especially" desire? Is it because this gift is often neglected due to the fact that it's unnatural, like speaking in tongue?

Or is it because it serves a vital but often neglected function which men and women deeply need for their strengthening, encouragement and comfort?

Reason #2—Obedience: Learning to prophesy is therefore the second reason why we need to have a Prophetic Ministry not only for people to experience the power of prophecy which can change an unbiblical mindset, but also to desire this gift with increasing eagerness as time goes by. As Paul concluded, "Therefore, my brothers, be eager to prophesy, and do not forbid speaking in tongues," we too should eagerly desire the prophetic gift and be eager to use it whenever we can, everything done in a fitting manner. This is an **OBEDIENCE ISSUE**; the more you're eager to use the gift in obedience to God's instructions, the more you'll be equipped to prophesy over others for their edification.

Reason #3—Outreach: There is a third reason why we need to grow in the prophetic gift and this is evident in what Jesus said in John 10:16: *"I have other sheep that are not of this sheep pen. I must bring them also. They too will listen to my voice, and there shall be one flock and one shepherd."* We who know the true shepherd because we know Him by His voice have a role in guiding other sheep that Jesus wants to bring into His kingdom. As we learn to hear and recognize the voice of God more and more, we'll be able to speak to people outside the church when we hear what God wants to say to them. Perhaps the best way to reach unbelievers who will be convinced of their need for God is when an appropriate prophetic word is released that brings a deep conviction in their hearts. This is an **OUTREACH ISSUE**;

we are called to be witnesses, relying on the power of the Holy Spirit to share our testimony wherever we can.

So be open to receiving the Prophetic Ministry which is now offered on the 3rd Sunday every other month. Better still, sign up with Pastor Perry for training to be a member of the prophetic team so you can be equipped to minister to others and continue to grow in faith as you get to know Jesus and His voice more and more."

CHURCH PLANTING

In 2012, we planted a church in Mississauga when a door was unexpectedly opened for us to use a meeting room to hold our Sunday Worship in the office of 'Power To Change' (formerly Campus Crusade For Christ, Canada).

Started by three members (Joseph Wee, Eric Wee, and Perry Soh) with the blessing of Life-Spring's leadership, it was quite a challenge in the beginning to have only a handful of people in attendance. "Who will show up today?" was the recurring question we asked ourselves, hoping to see a newcomer at the door each Sunday. Thank God that in spite of the small number, we were willing to continue with the expectation that newcomers would show up as long as the Lord was present and working in our midst.

We had been motivated to plant this church because of a vision which Eric Wee had shared with the church leaders several years ago. In the vision was a pair of hands handing Eric a sapling held in the palms (see picture). His impression was that the Lord was asking him to use the sapling to plant a church in the west end.

EMPOWERED FOR OUTREACH

Note: This vision picture was drawn by Perry's granddaughter, Olivia Soh.

As new people came along, mainly through word of mouth, it wasn't too long before the 30-seat meeting room began to fill up. Had Power To Change renewed its lease at the end of the year we would have continued to meet in this location. However, we were given two months' notice to leave. After a brief search in the neighborhood, backed by the members' fervent prayers, we were able to make a timely move. And in answer to our prayer for a bigger place with ample parking, God led us to a church building belonging to Salvation Army that could seat 150 in its sanctuary! This offered "Mississauga Life-Spring Christian Fellowship" more room to grow and to reach more people living in the west-end and in the Mississauga community. Praise the Lord for his goodness and provision!

ENCOUNTER WEEKEND

As an extension of our healing ministry, we have also been offering "Encounter Weekends" from time to time to minister not only to our members but also to Christians from other churches. Running from Friday evening through to Sunday afternoon, participants are required to stay over in a retreat center. In that quiet restful place, they are given the necessary teaching on inner healing before receiving personal ministry led by a trainer. It is always a joy for our ministry team to see participants set free from inner hurts and struggles that have affected their love for God and hindered their relationships with others. Many participants have discovered what a life-changing experience this has been. Our prayer is that this will be an on-going ministry so many more can be healed and restored to live in freedom in Christ and in the fullness of God's love.

CHURCH RENEWAL

In November 2016, we were approached by John and Lorraine, a couple representing Southland Church inviting us to its Church Renewal Weekend held in Steinbach, Manitoba. At that meeting, we were told that through Church Renewal, Pastor Ray and Fran Duerksen have been working with pastors of all denominations across Canada to bring renewal to the Canadian Church. As a result they have seen many lives and churches transformed. They believe that if the church is to be effective, it needs to be centered in prayer. And that prayer is the catalyst for renewal and transformation and the advancement of God's Kingdom.

Here are a few selected testimonies in their website (https://churchrenewal.com) confirming how pastors have been deeply impacted by participating in their Church Renewal Weekend:

- "The highlight for me was the prayer summit; 1100 people praying was nothing short of amazing. It gave me hope for the church. At Southland, prayer is their DNA. I encourage (everyone) to go to the next Renewal Gathering in October (26-28). Take as many of your leadership as you can."—Sr. Pastor, Promontory Church

- "The Church Renewal Leaders' weekend at Southland Church was a pivotal life experience for me. It was as though the light to my understanding of what God has been whispering to me and so many others at our church was turned on to full-power. Immersed in the life of Southland church helped provide clear vision for the journey becoming a God-centered, God-hearing, renewed Church."—Pastoral Assistant, Northside Foursquare Church

- "Nothing has impacted our church like the Set Free! Retreat attended by our key leaders. The high quality practical and relevant teaching sowed the seeds of transformational healing and wholeness which has grown and it's now bearing fruit in not only their lives but has rippled through the life of the church! We urge you to seize the opportunity to attend and discover for yourself the redemptive and restorative power of a God who longs for each church to reach its full potential. Set Free! Has mobilized us with a freshness and Spirit-filled renewal that we have been longing. Thank You."—The Church at Pine Ridge

What's noteworthy about Southland Church is that it now has a congregation of over 4,000 members even though it is located in a rural area in Steinbach with only a single hotel and a community consisting mainly of Mennonite farming families. How can one hotel accommodate so many guests coming to the church? It's the church families stepping up to host the guests assigned to each home whenever a Church Renewal Weekend is held in Spring and the Fall each year…and, based on our own experience, many guests have been warmly touched by their love and hospitality!

Since that meeting, 30 in our leadership team have gone to the Church Renewal Weekend and, given their testimonies and encouraging feedback, more of our leaders are planning to attend provided their registration are accepted within their intake quota.

As a result of Pastor Alvin's close association with Pastor Ray, a partnership has grown between Life-Spring and Southland Church. Since April 2017, we have been able to help organize and coordinate a series of Round Table meetings in Toronto, not only to promote the Church Renewal Weekend but also bring together pastors and leaders in different denominations with the aim of impacting the city through the renewal of more churches in Toronto.

In the beginning, we were blessed with Southland's generosity in hosting, at their expense, the weekly online mentoring sessions for the pastors who have been to their Church Renewal Weekend. In following Pastor Ray's instructive Church Renewal Manual during these sessions —starting with HEARING GOD in prayer and through meditating in His Word—we have found their approach to be quite effective in the mentoring/discipleship process. And this has motivated our pastors and elders to go through all the lessons themselves before passing them down to the next level of leaders…the deacons and life group leaders in our church.

By partnering with Southland through Church Renewal, Pastor Alvin has also been able to extend his network of pastors and church leaders in Toronto since accepting the role of Executive Director of MissionGTA. He stepped down as the Lead Pastor of Life-Spring in January 2019 and this has turned out to be a timely move to let a younger pastor, Gabriel Wee, step up in order to lead the next generation into the next season of renewal and growth!

A VISION-DRIVEN CHURCH?

In view of all we have witnessed and experienced so far in our journey as a church family, I am convinced that we ought to follow the "Diamond Vision" that God gave to Life-Spring in order to fulfill His will and purpose for the church.

STEP #1: It's God's will to save sinners wherever they are in the world (John 3:16): this is possible through **EVANGELISM** & personal witnessing.

STEP #2: It's God's will to heal the sick and deliver people from demonic oppression (Luke 9:1); this is possible through **HEALING & DELIVERANCE.**

STEP #3: It's God's will to raise disciples to carry out Jesus' mission in advancing God's kingdom (Matthew 28:19-20); this is possible through **EQUIPPING** & discipleship training.

STEP #4: It's God's will to demonstrate the Spirit's power so people's faith will rest on God's power rather than men's wisdom (1Corinthians 2:4-5); this is possible through preaching God's Word with **EMPOWERMENT**, accompanied by signs and wonders.

Everything undergirded by **INTERCESSION,** choosing to seek the counsel of the Holy Spirit through intercessory prayer, following the vision that God gave in order to flourish as a Spirit-filled, Word-centered church in the next season. That's the way for Life-Spring to go with God's guidance and favor!

CHAPTER 15

BE FRUITFUL AND MULTIPLY

As we approach the final milestone of our journey, it is prudent to ask ourselves: "Is there a higher purpose in God's plan for my life that I have yet to fulfill?" Even if we have achieved most of our life goals and served our earthly purposes, fulfilling all our responsibilities to the best of our ability in the eyes of our loved ones and people who are close to us, it's a question we need to ask ourselves to make sure we have ultimately been living according to God's perfect will for us.

In light of what Jesus said to his disciples as He approached the end of His journey on earth, we ought to bear in mind what He considered to be the most significant work that will leave a lasting legacy after we are gone.

What did Jesus say to His disciples that will help us see what is close to His heart? To do what really counts for the sake of others who come after us?

"I am the true vine, and my Father is the gardener. He cuts off every branch in me that bears no fruit, while every branch that does bear fruit he prunes so that it will be even

more fruitful...This is to my Father's glory, that you bear much fruit, showing yourselves to be my disciples...You did not choose me, but I chose you and appointed you to go and bear fruit – fruit that will last."(John 15:1-2,7-8,16)

Notice what was uppermost in Jesus' mind as He spoke these parting words to the disciples at this juncture before heading to Jerusalem where He was to be crucified?

Fruitfulness and fruit that lasts. Might this have to do with God's very first words to Adam and Eve after God had created the heavens and the earth in the beginning? *"Be fruitful and multiply, and fill the earth and subdue it."*(Genesis 2:28, RSV)

We know from the gospel message that everyone who chooses to believe in Jesus has an eternal destiny. *"For God so loved the world that he gave his one and only Son, that whoever believes in him shall not perish but have eternal life."*(John 3:16) Jesus came to fulfill the Father's will, sacrificing His life on a cross in order to save sinners from the condemnation of sin and death. So we who have received His salvation ought to bear witness to what God has done in our lives that others hearing this good news may also be saved.

Jesus further said to His disciples before his ascension into heaven, *"But you will receive power when the Holy Spirit comes upon you, and you will be my witnesses in Jerusalem, Judea and Samaria, and to the ends of the earth."* (Acts 1:8). With the empowerment of the Holy Spirit this is something all believers can do. It's my conviction that every follower of Jesus ought to obey His last words—relying not so much on self but wholly dependent on the Holy Spirit —to tell others about God's love and His plans to bless and prosper those who believe and are saved. For this was what the God of Israel said to his people through His prophet Jeremiah while they were living in exile in Babylon, *"For I know the plans I have for you, plans to prosper you and not to harm you, plans to give you hope and a future. Then you will call upon me and come and pray to me, and I will listen to you. You will seek me and find me when you seek me with all your heart."* (Jeremiah 29:11-13)

I believe the fruit that Jesus had in mind was for His disciples to reproduce what He had imparted to them so they could continue His mission in order to save people all over the world according to God's will. Time and again, we're reminded of these final instructions He gave them: *"All authority in heaven and on earth has been given to me. Therefore go and make disciples of all nations, baptizing them in the name of the Father and of the Son and of the Holy Spirit, and teaching them to obey everything I have commanded you. And surely I am with you always, to the very end of the age."* (Matthew 28:20)

In other words, as His followers, we are to reproduce ourselves by sharing our faith in Jesus with the intent to lead others to Christ wherever we may be in the world.

As I reflect on my journey as a follower of Christ, it is clearly by God's grace that I have survived the challenges I faced at different stages of my life. It is also evident to me that it is His sovereign hand upholding me that has enabled me to enjoy the numerous accomplishments and victories, both personally and in the ministries I was involved in. For this reason, I am most grateful for the way God has guided me, helping me to stay on course by engaging and serving with others in the work of His kingdom through the church. To change, renew, strengthen and equip me by **HIS SPIRIT** and through **HIS WORD** so I could be a fruit-bearing branch. To God be the glory for all the work He has done in Catherine and me, enabling us to love, teach, minister to and encourage the people He brought along the way.

NATURAL AND SPIRITUAL REPRODUCTION

In our own family, we have been richly blessed with the gift of natural fruitfulness. Catherine and I are thankful to have two sons through whom we have gained two daughters-in-law, Lynnette and Rosanna, and 12 grandchildren, Megan, Mikayla, Jacob, Evan, Elianna, Elliott, Nathaniel, Abigail, Olivia, Caleb, Tobias and Amelia. [2+2+2+12=18]. We have seemingly multiplied according to God's original plan! Thank God, everyone in the family is a believer growing in faith and in the knowledge of Jesus Christ.

The Lord had impressed upon my heart years ago to claim the following Scripture as His promise for our family:

"As for me, this is my covenant with them," says the Lord. "My Spirit, who is on you, and my words that I have put in your mouth will not depart from your mouth, or the mouths of your children, or from the mouths of their descendants from this time on and forever," says the Lord. (Isaiah 59:21)

With God working through three generations in our family, I am confident that we will see more natural and spiritual reproduction ahead.

In addition, we have also had the privilege to minister and connect at a deeper level with certain individuals who have acknowledged Catherine and me as spiritual parents. These spiritual sons and daughters have encouraged us to maintain our relationship with them no matter how long or far away they are from us. Fruit that lasts is what we expect to see when God continues to work in us and in them to will and to act according to his good purpose.

One Sunday, a sister in church, brought a printed article that I had written in an issue of the MSBC Newsletter* (Vol 14, Issue 4, Winter 1995). I did thank her not knowing why she had brought such an old article to me. But as I read the words again, I felt a strong stirring within me. And that's why I decided to include this article below because it re-affirmed my conviction that the Gospel of Jesus Christ ought to be shared by all committed Christians as often as possible with their fellow men.

CALLED TO BE WITNESSES

"As a church, we must keep our focus on evangelism since we are called to proclaim the gospel so that others hearing the good news might believe and be saved.

However, the word evangelism can evoke a neutral or even a negative response within the church. The general feeling

---

* This newsletter was later discontinued and hasn't been seen for many years.

is that we have neither the gift nor the training, so we simply let others do the job. The result is that there is little evangelistic activity even though many are aware from the Scriptures that they must share their Christian faith.

In His last words to the disciples before He ascended into heaven, Jesus said, *"But you will receive power when the Holy Spirit comes on you; and you will be my witnesses in Jerusalem, and in all Judea and Samaria, and to the ends of the earth."* (Acts 1:8). This is our commission from the Lord Himself that we are to be His witnesses. We each have our story to tell concerning our salvation. Nobody can tell your story better than you can. Nobody can reach the same circle of people you're in contact with in your everyday life. If you will not speak of Christ to these people, who will?

To be a witness is to testify about something you have personally heard, seen, or experienced. If you were speaking to someone whom you know (like a neighbor, a colleague, or a classmate) and you saw a need in the person which you could relate with, how difficult is it for you to disclose to the person how God had helped to meet that need since you received Jesus Christ as your Savior; and how His grace has been sustaining you day after day. If you haven't done it before, you should give it a try. It may surprise you that you can speak with such conviction because it was your own personal experience. Let it come spontaneously during the conversation and this would make you a witness to the living reality of Christ in your life.

A personal testimony, however, is only a testimony and it may not influence another person to seek after Christ. We need the power of the Holy Spirit to convict the heart and this is what our Lord Jesus promised when He said: *"But you will receive power when the Holy Spirit comes on you."* Success in witnessing, then, is simply sharing the gospel in the power of the Holy Spirit and leaving the results to God.

Think what a great impact MSBC will have in the community if every member is actively and regularly speaking out as a witness for Christ. Consider the contribution we can make to the Kingdom of God when souls are saved through the work of the Holy Spirt at our workplace, in our community, in all of Toronto and beyond. Pray that God will give us ample opportunity to do so."

Yes, we're all called to be witnesses! As the apostle Paul spoke so plainly, *"How, then, can they call on the one they have not believed in? And how can they believe in the one of whom they have not heard? And how can they hear without someone preaching to them? And how can they preach unless they are sent? As it is written, 'How beautiful are the feet of those who bring good news!"* (Romans 10:14-15)

REPRODUCTION AT LIFE-SPRING

Looking at fruitfulness within the church, we do see much fruit and generational growth among the adult members and young people whose lives have been radically changed as a result of our focus and reliance both on the WORD and the HOLY SPIRIT. Praise God, we now have a younger generation of leaders taking over from the older generation who have willingly passed on the baton. With the Holy Spirit living and working in them, we believe as the saying goes that "What is now our ceiling will be their floor" in the years ahead.

A good example is Gabriel Wee who grew up as a baby in church, served as a pastoral intern while studying at Tyndale Seminary, and is presently serving as the Lead Pastor of Life-Spring. Another example is Ryan Seow who also grew up as a baby in church, served as a pastoral intern while studying at Tyndale Seminary, went to Fuller Theological Seminary for his PhD studies on Missions before returning to serve as an Associate Pastor; he now leads our life groups while teaching part-time at Tyndale Seminary. A third example is Aldous Cheng, who also served as a pastoral intern while studying at Tyndale Seminary; with the in-house training he received in healing and deliverance, he was assigned as an Associate Pastor to teach and organize most of our H&D classes.

It's our hope and prayer that we will see more and more three-generation families at Life-Spring—children, parents and grandparents—worshiping and serving together to advance God's kingdom in the days ahead.

CONCLUDING WORDS

As I was pondering over what I could say as a concluding word in this last chapter, a Scripture and an old favourite hymn came to mind.

Listen to what King Solomon, the wisest man who ever lived, gave as his final word: *"Now all has been heard; here is the conclusion of the matter: Fear God and keep his commandments, for this is the whole duty of man. For God* will bring every deed into judgment, including every hidden thing, whether it is good or evil." (Ecclesiastes 12:13-14)

Listen also to the words of Fanny J. Crosby, an American mission worker who wrote more than 9,000 hymns even though she was blind from childhood:

> All the way, my Savior leads me
> What have I to ask beside?
> Can I doubt His tender mercy?
> Who through life has been my guide?
> Heavenly peace, divinest comfort
> Here by faith in Him to dwell
> For I know whate'er befalls me,
> Jesus doeth all things well.
> For I know whate'er befalls me,
> Jesus doeth all things well.
>
> All the way, my Savior leads me
> Cheers each winding path I tread,
> Gives me grace for every trial,
> Feeds me with the living bread.
> Though my weary steps may falter,
> And my soul a-thirst may be.
> Gushing from the rock before me,
> Lo! a spring of joy I see;
> Gushing from the rock before me,
> Lo! a spring of joy I see.
>
> All the way, my Savior leads me
> O the fullness of His love!
> Perfect rest to me is promised
> In my Father's house above.

> *When my spirit, clothed immortal,*
> *Wings its flight to realms of day,*
> *This my song through endless ages:*
> *Jesus led me all the way;*
> *This my song through endless ages;*
> *Jesus led me all the way.*

I pray these words will also resonate in your heart and encourage you to confidently commit your life to God all the way. For *"We know that in all things God works for the good of those who love him, who have been called according to his purpose. For those God foreknew he also predestined to be conformed to the likeness of his Son that he might be the firstborn among many brothers. And those he predestined, he also called; those he called, he also justified; those he justified, he also glorified."*(Romans 8:28-30)

All the way heading towards our final destiny! All the way as we wait for the Blessed Hope, the promised return of Jesus Christ, our Savior and Lord!

Made in the USA
Columbia, SC
07 September 2020